Echoes
FROM A HILL FARM

ILLUSTRATIONS BY
RICHARD STEINBOCK

• *Carnival Press* •
Northampton, Massachusetts

Echoes
FROM A HILL FARM

Susan Palmer Gleason

Carnival Press
351 Pleasant Street, Suite 277
Northampton, Massachusetts 01060

© 1989 by Susan Palmer Gleason

First published as a Carnival Press paperback

All rights reserved

Printed in the United States of America

No part of this book may be used or reproduced
in any manner whatsoever without written permission
except in the case of brief quotations embodied
in critical articles and reviews.

Most of these essays were previously published in
The Shelburne Falls and West County News

91 90 89   4 3 2 1

Library of Congress Catalog Card Number 89-61198

ISBN 0-9622435-9-0

Contents

Acknowledgments vii

Introduction ix

Map xiii

THE FARM

The Ten-Mile, Late-Night Cattle Drive 3   A Neighbor Passing Through 10   The Art of Naming a Dairy Cow 11   Harrowing 14   Seek and Ye Shall Not Find 15   Mr. Brown's Taxes 16   Finding Water 19   A Skunk at Night 21   Time for "Going Out" 22   Buying Milk 24   Faith and Ambition 25

THE COMMUNITY

Auctions and Tag Sales 29   A Sound in the Night 34   The Grandmother Rose 35   Images of Women 37   The Sad Ones of the Season 39   Waiting in Line at the Grocery Store 41   Reluctant Suspicion 42   Winning the Big Race 44   Ancestors for Sale 46   Evolution of Rubbish Disposal 48   Suburbia Comes to the Hill Towns 49   The Death of Pat Smith 52

THE INDIVIDUAL

A Kite to Fly 61   Being Measured for Fitness 63
A Box of Procrastination 65   Chimes of Great
Resonance 67   Marking Pages 69   A Person Defined
by Numbers 71   The Art and Science of Walking 73
All Will Be Well 76

THE NATURAL ORDER

The Bird of Spring 81   Treatise on the Pig Potato 82
Something is Missing 86   The Traveling Blossom 87
A Wolf at the Door 88   The Rebellion of an
Old House 90   A Pumpkin on a Fence Post 92
A Place Where Life Was 94   A Horse Again 95

Acknowledgments

Most of these essays were printed in the *Shelburne Falls and West County News* in my column entitled "Out There Somewhere."

A sincere thank-you to Mike Bakalar, who as editor-creator of the *News*, welcomed a less-than-confident writer who walked into the newspaper office in 1981 with an essay about the naming of dairy cattle and a dialog on living with an aging car. That was the beginning of an association that brought me from occasional contributor to reporter to columnist. All but two of the essays in this book appeared first, in different form, in the *News*. Thanks also to Mike for editing this book.

Thanks to Debbie Schafer-Valvo, who offered rousing support; and to Larry and Virginia Michie, who have provided constant gentle encouragement since they purchased the newspaper in 1986.

I want to thank Tom Absher of The Writers' Hotel of Vermont College and Gene Zeiger of Amherst Writers and Artists for their knowledge, inspiration and generosity.

Introduction

Here in the northwest corner of Massachusetts, in the hill country above the Pioneer Valley of the Connecticut River, perch some small rural towns. Life here goes on in its quiet normal way, with births and deaths, with seasons passing and pot holes appearing in the roads as regularly as minor dissension occurs in local politics. We are not far from the old ways here, in Heath and Colrain, in Shelburne and Buckland, in Rowe and Ashfield, Charlemont and Hawley, Plainfield and Conway. I live in Heath with my family: my husband Walt, my sons Daniel and Glenn. Ours was a working dairy farm until we faced economic reality and sold the cows in 1987.

These small essays represent one person's experience of life in these hills and the particular view it offers of the world beyond. I have tried to share that experience with you. I hope in reading my words you can hear some echoes from my life: the clump of hooves of eight escaped heifers; the sound of the wind moving around a dead tree lying over a stone wall deep in the woods; a chortle of laughter from someone reading the headlines of a tabloid while standing in line at a grocery checkout; the squish of boots moving through wet grass as we investigate a pumpkin sitting on a neighbor's fence post; the din made by friends gathered to serenade beneath the window of a newly married couple; a bellow from the long-distance conversation of cow and calf, recently separated; and the firm rhythmic counting of a volunteer rescue group giving cardiopulmonary resuscitation to a dying man in the ring at a cattle draw.

Here then, echoes from a hill farm . . .

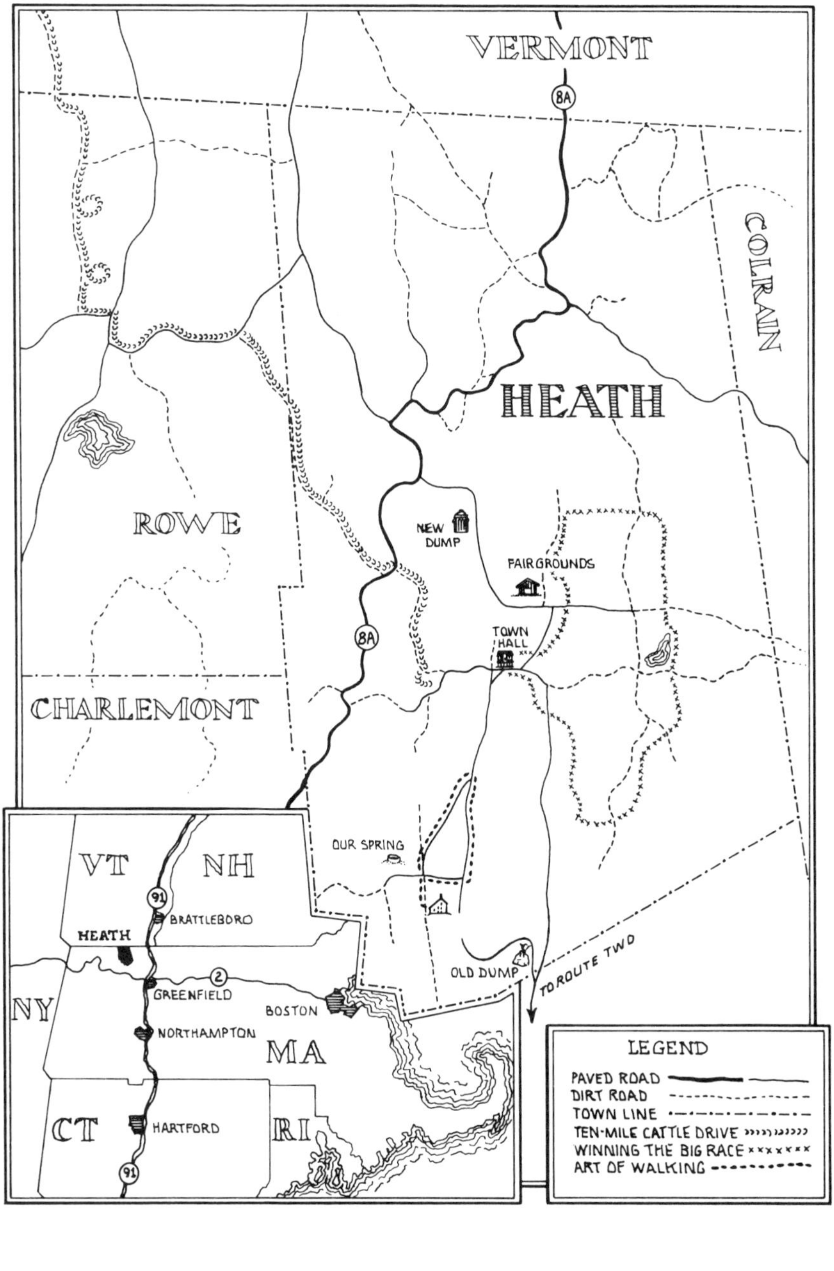
VERMONT
8A
COLRAIN
HEATH
ROWE
NEW DUMP
FAIRGROUNDS
TOWN HALL
CHARLEMONT
OUR SPRING
OLD DUMP
TO ROUTE TWO
VT
NH
91
BRATTLEBORO
HEATH
NY
2
GREENFIELD
BOSTON
NORTHAMPTON
MA
CT
HARTFORD
RI
LEGEND
PAVED ROAD
DIRT ROAD
TOWN LINE
TEN-MILE CATTLE DRIVE
WINNING THE BIG RACE
ART OF WALKING

THE FARM

The Ten-Mile, Late-Night Cattle Drive

It has been more than a year now. The puncture marks of cloven hooves must have vanished from the neat lawns of certain homes in Rowe. The people must have forgotten they were roused from early sleep or late night TV by strange sounds. Few will remember the barking dogs, thudding hooves and human calls of "Come bos, come bos." Perhaps the story can now be told.

It was our last summer at dairy farming (although we didn't know that at the time), and a golden opportunity seemed to have been presented to us: an offer of free pasture in Readsboro, Vermont, simply for fixing the fence around the land. Well, it sounded good. The eight heifers we had trucked there didn't seem interested in staying. They crossed unfordable rivers and jumped insurmountable fences, and we spent many summer evenings rounding them up. "Your cows are out," came to be a dreaded refrain we heard time and again over the phone. The heifers visited the town dump; they crossed the river and followed an old railroad bed to wind up a mountain away from where they belonged. Once, they even toured the main street of Readsboro. In the early fall, when some complication delayed the trucker who was to bring them home, they visited the Readsboro Elementary School, to the children's delight, but not to ours.

The Farm

The fateful evening started no differently from any other. It was after 8 P.M. and my husband Walt was trying to disengage himself from the TV in order to start the evening milking when the phone rang. I let him answer it. I thought he looked a little pale when he returned. "They're way up on Route 100," he said, "a quarter of the way home."

I didn't ask who "they" were. The family assembled, collecting pails of grain and flashlights and extra batteries. We set off, hoping the escaped animals would, this time, be somebody else's cattle. It was not to be.

Our options were not good. We could turn the cattle around and take them back down the mountain on Route 100, a busy road by cattle drover's standards, and onto the main street of Readsboro, then off on the side road and up the mountain to the pasture, where they clearly had no intention of staying. We could try, at this time of night, to find a trucker and a truck and then build a catching pen, capture the cattle and truck them home. Or, we could walk them home.

Faced with eight escaped Holstein heifers a long way from their pasture and a longer way from home, we knew the unruly beasts could not be relied on to stay in the pasture. We decided to walk them home, a distance of 9.1 miles through Whitingham and Rowe to a pasture in Heath. It was well after 9 P.M. that autumn evening when we started the drive.

We set off in a somewhat orderly manner with Walt leading the way, shaking a pail of grain and calling "Come bos, come bos." He was followed by the cattle in more or less single file, with the lead animal trying to thrust her head into the pail at each step. There was the occasional follower who would wander off to check out an apple tree on someone's lawn. She would have to be surrounded and driven back to the group by the two people walking behind the herd. The whole scene was lit by the headlights of the Toyota bringing up the rear. Sometimes a heifer would jump away from the others, four feet off the ground, tail straight in the air, spine twisted in that contorted way that makes you think that any self-respecting cow would never again be able to straighten herself out. Somehow she always does.

We had left Whitingham behind us and were in Rowe when we paused to rest and assess the situation. We were doing well, but at this rate it would certainly be after midnight when we reached our goal. And back at home there was a whole herd of cows waiting for somebody to milk them. Here is where we made a strategic error, for we sent Walt home with the car to do the milking and to gather the fencing supplies we would need to secure the heifers in their new pasture whenever we reached it. The boys and I moved on with the heifers, Glenn shaking the pail and calling; Dan and I bringing up the rear, our flashlights only partially penetrating the darkness.

As we plodded onto Potter Road I was lulled by my childhood memories of the terrain. In those days, Potter Road was bounded by stone walls, my father's wood lot, Ben Bjork's sugar bush, and a steep bank giving way to blueberry bushes. In those days, there would have been little to distract cattle being driven through, and indeed there would have been nothing surprising in cattle being moved there. But times had changed. We still found remnants of stone wall and while my father's woodland seemed unchanged, it soon became clear that the Bjork farm had been invaded and taken over by suburbia.

The Farm

We managed to keep the cattle off the lawns of the first homes we came to and were almost through this gauntlet of civilization when two dogs erupted from the darkness near a newly built house and rushed at the cattle, who turned and stampeded a mile back in the direction from which we had come.

The boys ran off after the cattle and I forced my tired legs toward the house to try to negotiate a stop to the canine hostilities. It took a long time to explain a cattle drive to the people. They didn't seem to know about cattle or understand why the dogs should be restrained. Communication was difficult—perhaps because of my tiredness, or because of theirs. (The man had been laying cement block all day, he said, and the woman had been firing off a shotgun at the Yankee Atomic Plant. Her arm hurt, she told me. I didn't ask if she was a guard or a demonstrator. At that point, I didn't want to know, although I have wondered since.) But they seemed suspicious of me for some reason. It did no good to try to explain that my parents were near neighbors; people in suburbia don't know other people a few acres away, and don't want to. But they brought the dogs inside and I only had to go about a half mile along the road before I met the boys bringing the cattle back.

We were exhausted by the time we got to the end of Potter Road. After all, we had traveled it twice. We turned onto Ford Hill Road and headed toward the east, and home. But most of the grain had been lost or eaten out of the pail. My back ached and my right leg was having trembling spells every few minutes. The heifers didn't follow the nearly empty pail with the enthusiasm they had shown for a full one.

We were within a few hundred yards of Leshures Road,

nearly within sight of the road to Heath, when the cattle decided they had had enough of all this. All eight of them turned and headed for the woods.

"Run, Mom, run! Get ahead of them! If you would run we could stop them!"

I could limp; I could hobble; but by this time I couldn't run. It took only seconds for the animals to get by me and vanish into the darkness of the woods.

It is a miserable feeling to be crashing through the woods at 11 o'clock at night with an inadequate flashlight, branches and briars reaching out to grab at you, in pursuit of a group of renegade cattle you can only hear. It wasn't long before both the cattle and my sons in pursuit of the cattle had outdistanced me. The woods became a very quiet and very dark place.

It didn't help much that I should know these woods well. I grew up very near to where I was now standing gasping for breath, my left leg in the embrace of a blackberry bush and my right foot sunk nearly to the ankle in bog. If cattle and drivers continued in a northerly direction we could wind up on my parent's property without ever leaving the woods. I certainly knew the dimensions of my predicament. If I could get cattle, sons and my own decrepit body out of the woods I would know exactly where we were and, with any luck, could head the drive again toward Health. But I didn't even know where cattle and sons were.

It was a time for reflection. When we decided that the escaped cattle would not stay in their Vermont pasture and we began to move them toward home, I had had fantasies of a handsome stranger coming by and offering us $500 per head for the critters. About the time the dogs had stampeded them back along the way we had already come I had

The Farm

altered my dream and would give the cattle away to anyone who wanted them, handsome or not. I had now reached the stage where I was willing to pay $500 per head to anyone who would take them off my hands.

I unwrapped myself from the berry brambles and squished on through the bog, listening and calling. It seemed forever before I heard an answer away off to the west, or where I imagined the west to be. "Oh, no," I thought. "Do we have to travel Potter Road again?"

Dan appeared from the darkness beside me and together we moved toward the sound of the calling. Glenn was with the cattle, who had, for the moment, stopped stampeding. They were leaning against a fence, conversing with a couple of white horses in the pasture beyond. Because of the fence, we couldn't even get the beasts back onto Potter Road. We would have to take them out through the woods. We were out of grain to lure them and I wasn't sure I could get through the woods without getting confused and going the wrong way. Glenn was sure we could do it.

We turned off our flashlights so we could pick up any clue of direction from the sky. Then, surrounding the cattle as best as three people can surround eight critters, we set off. For some reason the cattle moved for us, although at a pace much faster than I would have chosen. Again we were punished by the woods obstacles as we ran. I wondered when the cattle would tire of all this running and if it would be before or after I collapsed in exhaustion. At that pace we soon came out of the woods, and onto somebody's lawn, of course. But I knew where we were. And even the cattle were slowing down as we turned our way again toward home.

Walt rejoined us, unimpressed with the short distance we

had gained while he was home milking, but bringing a full pail of grain and the car to provide headlights.

I don't remember much of the rest of the journey. I know Dan, who had put in a full day of hard labor at his orchard job, collapsed in the back of the car and went to sleep. Glenn and I took turns walking behind the critters, rounding up any stragglers, or running ahead to block animals from turning off along the way. They seemed tired and thirsty now, not the wild bovines of a few miles back. And the car headlights seemed to help keep them in the road.

It was 1 o'clock in the morning when we reached a family pasture at Long Hill in Heath. I tried not to think of the next day, with Dan being obliged to go to work, Glenn to school, I to my job, and Walt, having just finished evening milking and a long hike, having to start milking all over again. We still had a half hour of fence building before we could leave the cattle and go home to bed. While our offspring slept in the car, Walt set fence posts and I strung wire. Then we headed home.

We had covered more than ten miles, counting dog stampedes and woods exploration. We had driven cattle where cattle had not been for years. We had left behind disturbed dogs and marred lawns, raided apple trees and puzzled suburban dwellers. We had built a fence by flashlight and collected our tools, leaving the heifers in new pasture. We figured they would stay there in contentment for a few days—especially if they were as tired as we were.

OCTOBER 1987

A Neighbor Passing Through

The planet Mars is closer these days. It shines as a clear red–gold light high in the Southern sky. Glenn, the family astronomy enthusiast, pointed it out to me during a rare break in the hazy, muggy, rainy stuff that has passed for weather in the last few weeks.

The ancients would have taken its approach to our earthly orbit as a bad omen. Their predictions would probably have run to violence and hardship, since Mars was the god of war.

It would be easy to take a dim view of the meaning of a planet's brighter presence in what we think of as "our" sky, since life in the farm orbit seems to be wobbling a bit anyhow. The Southern farmers have no crops to harvest because of the drought. The financial situation for most farmers in the Northeast is bad, and the attitude in Washington is less than helpful.

Farmers, of course, tend to feel picked on. I guess if you have to contend with whatever the weather throws at you, battle this season's bugs, and work with the unpredictability of mechanical devices, you have no patience left to expend in human circles—on unsympathetic politicians, for example, or uncaring bankers. I'm reminded of the chorus in the old song: "The Farmer is the one who feeds them all."

I'm taking Mars as a good sign, though. It is a beautiful thing to see glowing in the summer sky. And, in a pragmatic sense, to be able to see anything up there is an indication of clearing weather. Maybe we can get some haying done. Between mechanical disaster and bad weather we have done a scant amount of summer's most important work.

So I'm holding out for optimism. Our grass is green and thick and will make good hay, if we ever get it dried and in the barn. The hot muggy days and nights have made the corn grow. Pasture has been ample for the cows. Mars has its cycle and we have ours. Our orbit moves from spring to harvest time and back through the long winter to spring again. A visiting planet is just a neighbor passing through.

The Farm

AUGUST 1986

The Art of Naming a Dairy Cow

I wandered down to the milkroom to get milk for dinner. Hanging on a nail by the bulk tank was a note Walt had left for the inseminator. It read: "Two cows to breed. The one without horns is 'Horns'. The one with horns is 'Spot'."

He didn't say so, but both cows, like all good Holsteins, have spots.

There seems to be nothing planned or rational about the naming of cows. When I was a child, our family had two milk cows. The mother, a black Jersey cow with curved horns and an unsettled disposition, was named "Big Stupid." Her daughter was "Little Stupid." Of course "Little Stupid," due to the influence of her Guernsey father, grew to be much larger than "Big Stupid." Both were reasonably intelligent animals.

These days a cow's name is not a private matter between the farmer and the cow. Besides the inseminator, we have the milk tester. It is on the first visit of the milk tester, after a cow produces her first calf and joins the milking herd, that

The Farm

the christening ceremony occurs. Dawn, the milk tester, weighs the milk from each cow and takes a sample to be sent off for testing for butterfat content.

"What's the name of this cow?" she asks.

"Well, she doesn't have one yet."

The tester stands, pencil ready, and Walt thinks. At this time any name can descend on a helpless cow. Sometimes the farmer doesn't have enough imagination and sometimes he has too much. Sometimes the name is fine but circumstances change and the name becomes inappropriate. That's what happened to "Horns." She had a fine set when she was named but she used them too much and so had to undergo surgery for everyone else's safety.

I don't seem to be around often when cows are named, which is a shame because I could think of some good ones. A lot of my friends would like cows named after them. Occasionally a cow will remind me of an enemy. I could think of some creative names then.

So Walt thinks and the tester waits and some sort of name occurs. We have "Skinny" and "Short Legs" and "Fuzzy" and "Limp Horn" as descriptive names. We have "Wild One" and "Demon" and "Bitchy" as psychological profiles. We have "Dawn" because Walt named a cow after the milk tester, and "Sue" because he decided to salute me. If we have purchased a cow, he will name her after the dealer— an easy way to remember the value of that seller's wares. Rarely will he choose a conventional cow's name, like "Bess" or "Ruth" or "Bonnie."

Walt selects the name and Dawn enters it on the cow's permanent record. She sends her report and the samples to Cornell University, where they are fed to a computer who swallows the information and ruminates on it. The result of this electronic cud-chewing is a Dairy Herd Improvement print-out. These sheets tell you more about each cow than you wanted to know. They tell you her age, how many calves she has had, whether she is now giving milk, how much milk she gave in the last 365 days, how much milk she has given in her lifetime, what percentage of her milk is fat, how much money you got for her milk, how much she ate, how much what she ate cost you, and on and on. The computer even digests the inseminator's records and tells you if the cow is pregnant. Only one thing the computer can't handle—a cow's name with more than six letters.

So Dawn says, "What's the name?" and Walt says, "Let me think."

Walt comes up with something and Dawn says, "That's more than six letters."

So, like J.P. Morgan and ee cummings, a lot of our cows go by initials. We have "L.H." for "Limp Horn," and "F.B." for "Fat Belly," and "B.H." for "Black Heifer." And we have "U.P.A." "U.P.A." stands for "Unadulterated Pain in the Ass." "U.P.A." is, by cattle people's standards, a beautiful cow. She is also an intelligent cow, a curious cow, and, above all else, a hungry cow. She figures out how to open doors best left unopened. She's the first to escape the pasture and check out the new hay or the oatfield, or heaven help us, the neighbor's garden. She once drank a whole pail of iodine solution intended for udder wash, thus taking in her lifetime requirement of that trace mineral. Oh, another thing, she gives milk. A lot of milk. Our most productive cow is the one we gave the most offensive name.

Harrowing

I went out to the field where Walt was harrowing, tilling what had been corn field, ready to plant grasses for future hay crops. The soil moved softly beneath my feet. It was breaking up well, despite the days of rain that had encouraged weed and wild grass growth since it had been plowed. This is old land, tilled many times in the last 200 years or so.

I stooped to pick up an object by my feet. It was a rusty spike, large and pitted with years of lying underground. I showed it to Walt as he leaned down from the John Deere 2510 tractor that pulled the heavy disk harrows. It came from a spike tooth harrow, he thought. The harrow spike came to the surface with the new tilling, a reminder of the old technology, when people drove horses or oxen pulling the older style, flat harrows.

And that is what harrowing is, a stirring up of the old land to prepare for the future. You don't know what you may find when you start the process.

It's like removing a damaged plaster ceiling in an aged house. You can see the heavy beams that support the house and be reminded of the chestnut tree that provided solid timber in the days before the blight crippled the species. You might find an old iron hook or two embedded in the beams, hooks used by the settlers to dry produce or to store furnishings above the action of daily life.

Harrowing is like walking in the woods in this season, looking for timber trees or candidates for future firewood, and being alerted by the smell of lilacs to an old cellar hole where people once lived. You can sit on the edge and examine the pile of bricks that was once a chimney and you can try to figure out where the kitchen was and which of the nearby stone walls supported the structure of the barn.

We plan and work for the future. If our eyes are open, we will find clues to the past at the same time. We see our actions as part of a continuing process. Past then becomes part of future.

JUNE 1988

Seek and Ye Shall Not Find

I went to the woodshed Sunday in search of a garden rake and found a cowbell hanging from a peg by its worn leather strap. It spoke softly to me each time I bumped it as I prowled around looking for the rake. If someone had asked me for a cowbell, I would have said we probably owned one. I might even have looked in the woodshed. But I wouldn't have found it; I would have found the rake.

Walt received a letter last week that was written so obliquely he couldn't understand it. There was a reference to an article in a three-year-old town newspaper. The writer of the letter had been hopelessly optimistic about being understood. Nobody could remember the article, and, while it is possible that a copy of that particular issue lurks somewhere in our house, we don't know where. We didn't even try to look for it. We have learned a lesson over the years: you find what you are looking for only when you are looking for something else.

I didn't find the rake on Sunday. Finally, Glenn stuck an old rake head onto a broken shovel handle and I went off to

The Farm

my task of planting strawberry plants where only burdock had grown.

While I smoothed the strawberry plot I thought about it all. I could go out and catch a cow and put the bell on her, thus making use of the cowbell while I still know where it is. Of course, our cows are not used to being followed by sound, even melodious sound, and the cow might be offended and run rampant. A cow with a new cowbell tries to jump over it, I'm told, in an effort to get away from the new sound. This adds nothing to her dignity.

I could search the house for the wallpapering kit, or a copy of "The Elements of Style," or a crank ice cream maker, hoping to come upon the three-year-old newspaper along the way. But I know that won't work. In our disorganized house, just the image of the newspaper on the edge of my mind would prevent me from finding it, even though I would be officially looking for something else.

I pondered this syndrome of missing objects as I raked and smoothed. Finally I attacked one dirt clod with so much vigor that my recycled tool broke again into two pieces.

Somewhere in the woodshed is a decent garden rake.

APRIL 1986

Mr. Brown's Taxes

Several people at work were very upset that our employer failed to issue W2 forms by the statutory deadline of January 31st. They want to file their Internal Revenue tax forms to start the process that they hope will bring them a Tax Refund. I wish them well. I'm not so anxious to get started on the project. For one thing, I'm too cheap to hire somebody to do my taxes. For another, the whirlpool of schedules, rules, and mathematics surrounding the filing of a farm tax return gives me a headache.

But there is one part of the project to which I am looking forward. The IRS puts out a publication, #225, "Farmer's Tax Guide," wherein resides Mr. Brown. When I do my farm taxes I get to find out what has been happening to Mr. Brown in the last year. Mr. Brown is the IRS's answer to Tom Swift and Nancy Drew. Things happen to Mr. Brown and to his farm and he gets to fill out the required government form to report these events. There is always drama in the life of Mr. Brown.

Several years ago, three of Mr. Brown's heifers were struck by lightning and killed. Now I have had experience in such disasters and I know how difficult a time this must have been for the Browns. (Yes, there is a Mrs. Brown, but her life is very dull, poor thing. She is usually bringing in non-farm income by working in a day care center or something. And she *never* fills out tax forms.) So we know that Mr. Brown has three dead heifers on his hands. The IRS doesn't tell us who discovered the tragedy and if the animals were found in time to salvage the beef. We don't know if the heifers were the daughters of Mr. Brown's best cows or if they were average heifers who had inconvenienced the Browns by escaping from the pasture with great regularity. Here is the mystery. We have to complete the plot from the way Mr. Brown fills in his tax forms. Nobody was able to save any meat, I deduce, because Mr. Brown does not list a salvage value in his report of the tragedy to the IRS. He

The Farm

does have some insurance on his cattle, because he reports an insurance payment. And, we are pleased to learn, not all of the heifers were hand raised by the Browns, who could have become fond of them and would have been all the more saddened by their demise. We discover that Mr. Brown purchased two of the heifers. We know this because he gets to depreciate them, not something one can do with cattle one raises. So he reports the deaths and deducts his loss in a different way for the purchased heifers than for one he has raised.

Sometimes Mr. Brown has a Bad Debt. Now this is the IRS's version of a Bad Debt. It means that someone owes Mr. Brown money and that person either died or moved away and Mr. Brown has decided that he will never see his money. Now when I say that I have a Bad Debt, it usually means there is a bill I am having a very difficult time paying off. But, as I said, the IRS is different. When Mr. Brown has a Bad Debt, he deducts it from his farm income as a lost cause and goes on about his business.

I'm anxious to find out what happened to Mr. Brown in 1987. Can he still claim investment credit for the "beef cattle feeding facility" he built in 1983? Did he dabble in the stock market in 1987 and lose his shirt? Has he been able to make his mortgage payments? Did he, like so many other farmers, go out of business last year? How much was he able to save? Or did he get some money from Willie Nelson's Farm-Aid? If so, how on earth will he report that income to the Feds? I don't want to do my taxes, but I do want to know what's happening in the life of Mr. Brown.

FEBRUARY 1988

Finding Water

We had a dry household last week, even though it rained often.

The problem started with a savage thunder storm on the weekend. There was plenty of sound and visual effects with the storm. Neighbors suffered damage from lightning. We didn't know we had a problem ourselves until Tuesday when the water pump ran but the faucets were empty. There was no water in the storage tank and no water coming in.

So it has been a week of cleaning the sap-gathering tank so we could haul in a water supply; of learning over again how to use a laundromat; of bathing less frequently, or not at home; of evening exploring expeditions to search out the location of the rupture in the water pipe.

Our water travels a long distance, carried by lead pipe from the spring to the house and barn. We rarely have problems with it, but when we do, it means a good hike just to identify the problem.

When a water supply line has been ruptured by lightning an ordinary person must turn physicist in order to solve the problem without digging up the entire length of pipe. I know next to nothing about physics and had to have it explained to me by my spouse.

"Why are we digging here?" I asked, inaccurately. Walt was digging—with an inadequate garden shovel. I was watching.

We had hiked along the faint dip in the terrain that still marks where the trench was dug to bury the pipe in 1942. We had passed through our pasture and pine woods and were now in the field below the neighbor's house. We would have as far to go again to reach the spring.

We had found a pine tree shattered by lightning but we had continued on to this spot, where we had done some token hocus-pocus with a forked branch from an apple tree—water witching. Now we were digging. It was a good enough place to dig but I didn't understand why.

So I got an explanation. If lightning hits the water pipe it will move along it until it reaches a splice. At that place there is a difference in pressure and the pipe will give way. The lightning knows more about physics than I do.

So we found a break in the pipe there in the field and we went home to see if water was now coming in. It wasn't.

There is physics in a force pump, too. When you have dug up a ruptured water pipe and repaired it and water still doesn't flow through the pipe you go into the cellar with a pump (ours is an antique hand pump that looks something like a bicycle tire pump) and you pump some of the precious water you have hauled up the water pipe. It meets the water coming down and it all comes together and starts the system working again. It's like an enema, I guess.

It was days before we had running water again. In the end we repaired two ruptures in the pipe at splices and created a new splice where the lightning had struck the tree, exploded along the ground and hit the water pipe. The pipe was not only ruptured in that spot, it was melted and gnarled.

So we were six days without water. Everybody got a refresher course in finding the spring and following the pipe line. We know which neighbors have long-handled shovels and how long it takes to fill a gathering tank from a roadside spring with buckets. I learned water conservation skills and a little practical science.

JULY 1988

A Skunk at Night

The weather has been warm and we have been sleeping with the windows open. We also have a dog. Now, those sound like two circumstances that have absolutely nothing in common. People do sleep with the windows open and people do have dogs. So what? Last night a third circumstance entered the equation which united the other two and created a dramatic situation. The third element in the plot was a skunk who wandered by, unconcerned with us or the dog.

Unfortunately the dog was not so uninterested in the skunk. Dog investigated skunk. Skunk sprayed dog. Sleeping people awoke and knew exactly what had happened.

It was too late to close the windows. We tossed and turned. I tried covering my head with a fat pillow. I tried suggesting to the dog (who, my olfactory senses told me, was lying beneath the bedroom window) that she go move in with the neighbors. She failed to comply. I suggested to the skunk that he or she go someplace considerably warmer. I don't know if the skunk obeyed. Probably not. Skunks are independent of human needs.

I forgot to roll up the window of my car last night. The dog has taken on the habit of jumping through open car

The Farm

windows and curling up on a nice comfortable car seat to sleep. She especially likes my car because it has soft seat covers of phoney sheep skin—the pelt of the dreaded Acrylic, I think. Anyway, that is where I found her early this morning. I have hung the seat covers out to air.

So I didn't sleep very well last night and the ghost of the confrontation continues to haunt my household. I predict my relationship with the dog will be a distant one for a few days. At least, it will be as distant as I can make it. She clearly has no such feelings. She wouldn't mind crawling into my lap right now. Border Collies are not lap dogs but somebody forgot to tell her.

So if anybody knows of an effective skunk repellant, I am definitely interested. Or maybe I need a good dog training device. Or a very large Air-Wick. Skunks, dogs and open windows are a very bad combination.

JUNE 1988

Time for "Going Out"

Making the decision was difficult. For me, it came after more than twenty-two years of life on a diary farm; for Walt after a whole lifetime of farming, of milking cows twice a day ever since he was in junior high school. We were burned out once; we lost our herd and buildings, but we gathered our resources and, with community support, rebuilt and started again with a new mortgage. But it wasn't working. The economics of trying to run a family farm in this age were against us. The margin between milk check and grain bill continued to shrink. So it was time to stop, to let go, to give up: "Going Out," to use the farmer's phrase.

The big trucks came three times last week to take away cattle. On Saturday more trucks came and we loaded the last of the animals. It was sad.

Our whole pattern of time is changing. The dog is confused; she doesn't know where the cattle are, nor does she understand why nobody is going to the barn, morning and evening, to milk. Walt is measuring his days by a time clock and somebody else's schedule. It will be different from pacing time by the rhythm of twice-a-day milking, or measuring the year by seasons full of farm duties dictated by the weather. After eleven years of full-time work off the farm "to support the cattle," my own life is changing, too. I need to reexamine my getting up and heading out to work. Before, it was to help keep us going as a farm. Now what is it for?

It was the time to "go out." For us it was a rare triumph of intelligence over tenacity. We don't give up easily. But there is virtue in being able to let go of a burden when the time comes. Once, it was appropriate to carry it, but that day has passed. It is good to leave the business honorably, good to start fresh.

But it will take a while to get used to it all, to appreciate our new wisdom and to understand who we are and where we are going. The other day someone called for information for the town street list and needed to know our "occupations." I don't know what she finally wrote down. For the first time I was unable to answer the question.

The Farm

MARCH 1987

Buying Milk

I stood there in the middle of the convenience store, a jug of milk in my hand and I looked at it ruefully.

It seems such a simple thing. "On your way home, stop at the store and buy some milk." But I felt uncomfortable and conspicuous. I had never done it before, you see. In all my years as purchasing agent for a household I had never bought milk.

Milk doesn't come from a store; it comes from cows—our own cows, feeding on our own land. It comes from beasts with names like Fat Face, Tiny, Skinny, Carol or Chicken. They are creatures as varied as any humans and as full of personality. But we had sold the cows and I was buying milk.

I looked at the price label on the jug: $2.09 for a gallon. I don't know milk prices in gallons. I know milk price by hundredweight.

A farmer selling milk gets about $13 for a hundred pounds of it. By the time the deductions have been taken out for transportation, for promotion, for cooperative dues and equity, for retroactive funding of the federal buyout program, the farmer is lucky if there is $10 per hundredweight left.

That's 10 cents per pound. A gallon jug holds eight pounds of milk. That means the farmer got 80 cents, the middle people got $1.29.

That's the American economy today, and that's why we sold the cows. The 80 cents wasn't enough to pay the grain bill, purchase seeds and fertilizer, repair worn equipment, and keep the farm going.

I stood in line at the cash register and thought about it all.

I wondered if people dealing illegal drugs feel half as uncomfortable as I did the first time I bought milk. I'll just have to get used to it.

Farming in a hilltown—struggling to get a good corn crop for silage in a short growing season, working to get the haying done before the rains—is a luxury few can afford these days. It will take a while for this family to get used to the change. It will be a relief for us, then, an easing of a burden.

The man ahead of me paid for his cigarettes and beer and moved along. I put the jug of milk on the counter and dug some money from my wallet. Nobody was staring. The cashier looked bored as she rang up the purchase. It was just an everyday sale for her, just routine.

I wonder how long it will be before I can feel the same about it.

APRIL 1987

Faith and Ambition

I almost didn't plant a garden this year. Every year I almost don't plant a garden. There have even been one or two years when I really didn't plant one. But usually it is just almost, a perennial near miss.

Planting a garden is an act of faith. It is also hard work. And after a long hard winter I am usually a little short of faith and ambition. But in some contradictory way the garden, which requires the investment of faith and effort, pays

The Farm

back by restoring faith and renewing effort. I don't know how it happens. I only know that I make a quick trip to the garden to pick a little lettuce or chard for a meal and I will end up weeding the beans, staking the peas, and stripping the extra limbs from the tomato plants. All the time I look around me at the growth of weeds and vegetables in astonishment and yet with recognition of a phenomenon I *knew* would occur.

It seems that if you plant things around here, they will grow. I know that inside myself, even though in early spring it is hard to act on that knowledge. All you have to do is stir the soil a bit, move a few rocks aside, put in some seed, and something will come up and thrive. The something may be pigweed and dock or a volunteer tomato plant—the heritage of last season's rotten fruit, but something will surely grow. That is life. And the bugs will come to eat from the things that are growing. And that's life too, although we value that life less than the vegetables that earn us blue ribbons at the fair.

So I planted my garden and it now contains vegetables: beets and turnips now beyond the stage of mere greens; cabbages folding in about their centers; green tomatoes; corn that was knee high days before the traditional fourth of July and now stretches nearly to my shoulder. True, some beans didn't germinate, the weeds are doing well, pretty white moths keep laying eggs on the cabbage, and the eggs turn into green worms that like to eat cabbage.

All in all, the garden has repaid my meager faith and weak ambition beyond what I deserved. I took on the task half-heartedly; the garden grew with full enthusiasm.

JULY 1988

THE COMMUNITY

Auctions and Tag Sales

Auctions and tag sales interest me. There is, of course, the challenge of acquiring somebody else's used goods for a reduced price. Like everybody else, I tend to remember the John Deere field chopper I purchased at farm auction for $750 when Walt had instructed me to bid up to $1400 for it. I tend to not remember the hanging lamp I purchased for $25 that was in such poor condition we couldn't use it.

More is happening at auctions and tag sales than the informal purchase of used goods. There is always something interesting going on, something or someone to observe and maybe laugh about, even if the joke lies only in my own behavior.

Each tag sale has its own character, according to what is happening in the family hosting it. Many village neighborhoods feature signs, homemade or printed, proclaiming that another family is tidying up or moving or simply trying to make good on some previous investments in collectibles.

There are also, of course, the "professional" tag sales. These are conducted at homes that feature a sale nearly every week, or at tourist businesses that use large parking lots on traveled routes to rent space to weekend entrepreneurs who hawk inexpensive jewelry or irregular goods purchased wholesale, as well as the gleanings from attic or shed.

I buy things at tag sales. Usually what I buy is not something I went looking for. I buy sneakers for Glenn, size nine and one-half, priced at $5 because each shoe is a slightly different color.

I buy tomato plants in season and garments in colors that happen to be unfashionable this year but suit me any year. Dan's guitar came from a tag sale, and Walt's winter coat.

Tag sales are fun, but auctions are better. Auctions come in several different varieties.

There is the charity auction. This lacks the personal touch of the tag sale or the household and farm auction. Usually you bring something to a charity auction and you buy something else. One day I bought a $300 skirt at a charity auction for $5. The whole thing got me thinking about value and values.

I picked the skirt from a table loaded with books, knick-knacks, a carving set or two, a pile of rolled-up movie posters and other odd items. I held it up against me to see if it might fit. I liked the color. It was well made, from a heavy napped beige fabric, and was fully lined. It looked perfect for a winter occasion requiring something more dressy than my usual pants. So I resolved to bid to a reasonable amount—$5 or $6.

There weren't many people my size there and the whole issue of size was clouded by what appeared to be a mislabeling inside the skirt.

So I got it for $5. As the runner carried the skirt to me she spotted the label and set up a loud cry. "It's a Valentino. It's a Valentino." I could only associate the term with a long-dead movie star. The woman beside me kindly explained something about high fashion and European sizing and the spending of hundreds, even thousands, of dollars for a single garment. Other people joined in to educate me about this particular designer. I believe Jackie Onassis was mentioned.

I found myself involved in strange daydreams about the skirt. It needed to be taken in an inch or two in the waist, something I'm fully capable of doing with any normal skirt. But should I tackle the job in a $300 skirt, to pick one of the more conservative estimates of my fellow auction-goers? I had better hire someone to do it right.

And what could I wear with it? When I first saw it and it was only a good warm skirt, I thought I could wear it with my nice coffee colored polyester blouse, the $4 one I got from Rethreads, the second-hand clothing store, when white tagged items were half price. Obviously, for a $300 designer item I had better buy a silk blouse. Maybe something in gold.

And where could I wear it? Even when it was only a good warm skirt lying on the table, I had never planned to wear it to the barn. I had thought I could wear it to work at the library on book discussion days. Now I wasn't sure about that. I might get book dust on it. Maybe I could get Walt to take me to the Plantation House. A designer garment deserves a gourmet environment.

Things were clearly getting out of hand. It was the same item on which I had decided to risk $5; the only change was in my perception of it. My bargain was going to be hard to live up to. And it would cost me a bundle. So I decided to forget Valentino and Jackie Onassis. I picked it up at an auction because I liked the color. I plan to wear it and enjoy it. I'm not going to bend my life out of shape to fit an auction skirt.

Household auctions are difficult to find these days. I remember the household auctions I used to attend as a

The Community

child. Personal effects of house, shed and barn were sold on the site at public auction. It was not the modern sterile auction hall, with carefully picked over selection from several owners presented in a sophisticated style of merchandising.

The home auction had a reality not to be found in the auction hall. It was a drama. If an estate was being settled, everyone knew it; they knew who had died and of what. If the family were moving, or giving up farming, everyone knew that, too.

Weather was a factor, truly a "character" in the drama of the day. I have achieved some outstanding sunburns at auctions and I have been chilled and rained on as well.

As a small child, I was issued a quarter to spend at the auction and I would wait anxiously for my opportunity, ignoring the furniture and bedding and merely looking at the toys and sleds or skis the auctioneer would hold up—those were far beyond my budget. There would be the usual old chair converted to a commode for an invalid, providing an opportunity for Mr. Call, the auctioneer, to tell his inevitable joke. There would be the chipped pitcher and washbowl that would bring an amazing price from an antique dealer, one of many who came with folding chairs and brimmed hats to bid up the prices on quaint items to the entertainment of those, like us, who came to buy good secondhand items at bargain prices.

Finally my time would come. Mr. Call would hold up a battered cardboard box and announce that here was a miscellaneous lot. He would fish out a limp little basket, a grimy beaded velvet pincushion, perhaps a small undefined mechanical object and ask in vain for someone to bid $2 or even $1? I would hold my breath. "It's a Klondike," my

32

father would whisper, "maybe a gold mine." I would take a deep breath and call out, as loudly as I could, "25 cents!" Somehow my voice was never very audible. Often I would have to wave my hand and repeat the bid.

To the auctioneer it was a miscellaneous lot—to us it was a Klondike. A Klondike was an adventure, not merely a purchase. Who knew what might lie at the bottom of such a box? A Klondike might contain a treasure; it might contain only junk. Usually the Klondike would be a disappointment. Sometimes a Klondike would contain something special, or perhaps an item or two that someone else in the audience wanted to acquire without the rest of the junk in the miscellaneous lot. It was a triumph to be able to sell some of the contents of a Klondike to others for more than you paid for the lot and still have something of use to take home.

The farm auction was even better than the household one. You got all the miscellanies of the household and all the variety of the farm. There were porcelain eggs used long ago by farm people to fake the hens into laying in the nests rather than on the ground; there were coffee cans and tobacco tins filled with screws and nails and bolts. There was worn farm machinery and old harness. The farm auction had all the best features of the tag sales and the more limited auction. There was weather and people and goods, the prime ingredients for entertainment and insight.

SUMMER 1986

The Community

A Sound in the Night

Cacophony, n. a harsh, discordant sound.
Tumult, n. 1. an uproar. 2. a state of confusion and agitation.
(*Oxford American Dictionary*)

In these parts, we have an old custom of extending a form of social nicety known as the "serenade" or "shivaree" to a newlywed couple. It is a form of respectable hoodlumism consisting of the gathering of a group of friends late at night beneath the bedroom window of the honored couple. The group is equipped with horns (hence another and even more old-fashioned term, "horning"), whistles, gongs and any other device that could be counted on to rouse the sleeping couple.

In a serenade, the neighbors come to call, essentially to bring good wishes once the attention of the honored couple has been captured. The unexpected guests bring refreshments and come inside to socialize a bit.

There are rumors of a time in years gone past when the serenaded couple refused to acknowledge the racket under the window. The legend says the serenaders returned every night for a week until the couple got up and let them in. I think the story is apocryphal, myself; there must be a limit to how many nights hard-working people are willing to stay up until 1:30 in the morning just to go visiting the neighbors.

Nobody remembers when the custom of the serenade started, but it seems to run in cycles. Sometimes it is popular, with many serenades in a season; then it dies down for a few years. For six years or so a four-foot mill saw leaned against a stump in our yard, abandoned by the folks who brought it to beat with heavy hammers at our serenade, waiting for us to take it on to the next one.

The custom is enjoying a revival in these times. A few years ago, friends and neighbors even chose the serenade as the appropriate way of observing a couple's fiftieth anniversary. But that was a special couple. Usually the racket is in celebration of a recent marriage, when the couple is young enough to survive and appreciate the turmoil.

Modern times have contributed technological advances to this noisemaking, of which the chainsaw is the most effective. A bullhorn "liberated" for an hour or so from a volunteer fire department is a nice touch, too.

Transplanted city people tend to be a bit surprised by the event, lulled into false serenity by tales of the peace and quiet of the country and by the reputation of the natives for stand-offishness and emotional restraint.

This weekend's honored couple had never heard of a serenade and responded to the din by reaching for the telephone to call the police and report a motorcycle gang gone wild.

"I didn't know what it was," said the bridegroom, "but I didn't think it would be *friends*."

SEPTEMBER 1986

The Grandmother Rose

They call it the Seven Sisters Rose, those people who remember and still care about the old-fashioned roses. But in our family it's called the Grandmother Rose. There is a

The Community

bush to be found at the homes of most of the descendants of one woman.

It's the usual old style rose, exploding into bloom in mid-June and fading out as soon. In its brief time of glory it displays a very different and somehow more stable blooming than the modern hybrid rose. The pink hybrid tea rose that I planted a while back, for example, suffered ill from an icy winter, and died back on one main branch to some ancestral point below the graft. Half the bush blooms a delicate pink, the other half rambles with vigor up the house, displaying crimson flowers. It is interesting, but somehow unsettling. I like the old style roses best.

The original name for the Grandmother Rose, Seven Sisters, was given because the buds open a vivid, deep pink and fade within a few days to near white. Thus each bush displays many different colored flowers at the same time.

The Grandmother for whom the bush was given its family name was a typical woman of her day, with a large farm family and a home business. Although she was disabled by a stroke long before grandmotherhood, she kept herself involved with life. She sewed with her good hand, pressing the fabric deep into her lap with the heel of her hand to hold it still while she forced the needle through. She took pleasure in her visitors and enjoyed an opportunity to sit out under the trees or to go as far as the barn when someone was available to help her walk.

She planted the first Grandmother Rose bush, no doubt from a root someone had given her. The family story is that she limped down the porch steps with a crutch to plant the bush. The family remembered. Seventy-five years or so later they still remember. And it's still the Grandmother Rose Bush.

The Community

When I was grafted into the family, I inherited the tradition. When our Grandmother Rose bush was destroyed by the puppy antics of a young Border Collie named Edgar, I felt as sad as everyone else. The yard seemed incomplete without it. Fortunately a grandchild of the original bush had started to spread and we were offered a root. Now, two years from the time we carefully transplanted the new bush, it is blooming with its characteristic multi-colored blossoms.

Some of us take our roots literally, I suppose, cherishing the physical and natural things that support our traditions. I'm not interested in written diagrams of family trees or endless conversations on the exact blood relationship between this and that member of a wide-spread clan. When it comes to family heritage, a rose bush has the kind of roots I can appreciate.

JUNE 1986

Images of Women

There are portraits on the wall in the domain of one of my health care people. One shows a person stripped to the barest reality of bone; one shows the person as a pattern of muscle over bone; one shows organs; and another shows the seemingly messy accumulation of nerves and circulation tubes which somehow resolve themselves into an orderly and functional beauty. They are painstakingly done and I find them works of art as well as works of science. But they

The Community

bother me. After a couple of visits to this healing place I asked about them.

"Why are they all men?" I said, waving my hand toward the wall from my prone position.

"There's a diagram of a woman's pelvis over here," said the therapist, pointing to an inset in the corner of one of the charts. Fortunately, I had observed that diagram previously, as I was now bereft of my glasses and operating on memory. I could barely see the wall, but I knew the pictures were there.

"But it seems that the men are whole and the woman is only a fragment," I objected. "Women are whole, too."

"The bone diagram looks to me like it has a male pelvis but the muscle diagram could be either sex," he said, not commenting on the diagrams of organs and nerves and blood flow, which were unquestionably male.

I remembered the muscle diagram. There were a lot of muscles on it. And it seemed to me that the muscles contained a man's body, with its higher center of weight and its straighter hips. I decided not to quarrel about it but to file the whole thing away, perhaps someday to understand it.

The anatomy charts weren't on my mind this week as I walked to the Artspace Gallery of the Arts Council of Franklin County to see an exhibit called "The Birth Project." The artist was Judy Chicago, a contemporary who made some unusual things. There was something a while ago about fur-lined teacups, I remembered. So I didn't expect "The Birth Project" to show pictures of quiet women with babes in arms, smiling mysterious smiles. It didn't.

The display went right to the mystery and left out the coy stereotypes. It showed wombs and birth canals and lactation, and centered on the universal experience of birth.

It wasn't quiet. It was beautiful. I was moved that Judy Chicago's explosive paintings had been given form in needlework by women who learned to crochet or embroider in the conventional way. Those women were used to making tablecloths or samplers or children's clothes. Now they were depicting creation, human and global, in pictures of women's experience.

So I'm thinking about it all—about the anatomy portraits and about "The Birth Project." I don't expect health care people to hang a Judy Chicago work on the wall for use in educating the ailing about what body part hurts and why. And an anatomy chart, no matter how beautifully done, even if we could find one of a woman, would be out of place in a contemporary art display centering on the experience and mythology of birth. It seems to me that in our lives we have both art and science. And we need images of women in both.

SEPTEMBER 1987

The Sad Ones of the Season

The odd ones, the unfortunates, become more visible this time of year. From Thanksgiving to New Year's Day they seem to increase in number and in need. As we rush around, meeting our social obligations, doing our holiday shopping, and simply pausing to enjoy the season, they are there.

Sometimes they are quiet and sad. Sometimes they are

The Community

loud and contentious. Our preoccupation with shopping lists and holiday invitations is interrupted by their presence. They shock or aggravate us. We drop coins in the Salvation Army bucket, but who wants to *see* the homeless? Or worse, who wants to hear them in their need?

"But I need an apartment. The newspaper says you have an apartment. What do you mean, do I have any children? My children were taken away from me in 1964!" screams a voice from a public phone booth.

We really don't want to hear.

Some are released mental patients. We don't want to see them, to try to understand them, to be startled by their behavior. We understand that the state mental homes were in terrible condition, we know these people must be somewhere—but here? In our sight? And are they taking their medications? Should we be afraid of them?

They come to public buildings for heat, for shelter from the weather, for restrooms. They are neither quiet nor tidy.

A badly dressed man sets his knapsack down too roughly in a public library, shattering a bottle of muscatel. The stench of cheap wine fills the place, ruining the festive atmosphere, negating the cheerful presence of holiday decorations and the hushed recording of Christmas carols.

The vandalism in public restrooms becomes increasingly senseless and bizarre. Someone stuffed a brand new 45 RPM recording into a public toilet (wrapper and sales slip found nearby), defecated on it, then flushed. The repair was difficult and aroused no feelings of Yuletide joy in the janitor assigned the job.

We go our ways, those of us able to arrange our lives and tend our affairs with some grace. We try not to look at the clumsy and inappropriate situations these odd people are living with. Why don't they go away? Or at least fade into the background? What do they want of us? Why bring this awkward, bitter gift of awareness into our secure lives? And why, of all times, at this season? Not all our holiday gifts are those we would have chosen.

The Community

DECEMBER 1986

Waiting in Line at the Grocery Store

You stand in line in a supermarket, peering over your loaded cart to assess the line ahead of you. It looks like a long wait. You shift from one foot to the other, you count the tiles on the floor, you calculate that if you removed thirty-seven items from your cart you could move over to the express line. The line moves slowly onward. You are almost at the counter now. You try to remember all the words to "When the Saints Go Marching In." You practice abdominal breathing. Then you see it. "Rabbit-faced Baby Has 10-inch Ears. Bucktoothed Mom Chomped Carrots While Pregnant!"

Good grief. Who believes that stuff? Who buys that ridiculous newspaper, anyway? "Stroke Victim Falls in Garden and is Eaten by Her Venus Flytraps!" "Heroic Mom Gives Self Caesarean, Stranded on Highway, She Uses Can Opener." (The baby lived, the woman died.) "Bearded Lady Sues Hubby for Making Her Hair Fall Out!" "Wife Cremates Her Husband With His Favorite Girlie Pix!" "Scratched Woman Sues Kitty Cat's Owner for 250 Grand!"

The Community

A co-worker recently brought one of those tabloids to work and I was able to do an in-depth study of the phenomenon. I was interested to find buried in the back a story datelined Bernardston, Massachusetts: "Beaver Bites Man!" But that was tame compared to the rest. I especially enjoyed the story headlined "UFO Aliens Helped U.S. Congress Write Constitution." The reasoning used to deduce that "fact" is that people needed help from beings with superior intelligence to do such a job. I guess that isn't an amazing attitude from an editorial staff that deals every day with such evidence of human intelligence as "Tammy Bakker Doll Made My Wrinkles Vanish Overnight!" and "Haunted Paintings Make Hundreds Ill!"

But I have decided these newspapers are good to have around. The journalism is questionable; the unintentional humor is priceless. What else can you do with "Hubby Eats Dog Food to Protest His Wife's Cooking!" but laugh? And why not laugh? Next to abdominal breathing it is the best way to pass time in the grocery check-out.

SEPTEMBER 1987

Reluctant Suspicion

My neighbors tell me they are missing a Christmas tree. It vanished during deer season and a suspicious trail led across their pasture toward the west, where the thief decided the tree was too heavy to drag and too large to fit in his living room, anyway. So he cut off a large chunk which he left under the electric fence, effectively short-circuiting the current.

It seems to me the thief heaped on the insult in sabotaging the fence as well as stealing the tree, but maybe I'm thinking ill of someone who deserves better. Perhaps the person who took the tree was just a poor old hunter who was lame and needed a staff to lean on as he made his weary way home to his wife and children.

I thought of the old story about a local character named Amos who had a shaky reputation in the areas of sobriety and honesty.

One evening Amos's neighbor was disturbed by an unusual racket from the hens and went out to see what was going on. The neighbor had got into the habit of sitting up nights due to a mysterious decline in numbers in the poultry flock. The chickens were spending the night in a range shelter, a tiny low building that to a non-poultry expert looks more like the house of Eeyore, the little donkey in the Pooh books, than a real farm building.

Anyway, the neighbor went out to investigate and there was Amos, bent over double inside the shelter, with a chicken in each hand and an open sack by his feet. "Why, Amos," said the neighbor in gentle surprise, "whatever are you doing here?"

"Looking for my horse," said Amos.

I think about Amos when I find things missing under suspicious circumstances. I work in a library. Librarians do make mistakes, but I find it hard to believe that we have lost all the books that are missing from the stacks.

Books about certain subjects tend to vanish more than others. For example, books about witchcraft, ghosts and palm reading disappear often. Do they levitate away? Why

The Community

The Community

do books about natural childbirth have to be replaced so often? They don't wear out, they simply go.

Automotive repair books such as "How to Fix Your 1978 Chevy Truck" are another type of item that doesn't stay around. Books about how to write resumes go out often, return seldom. Where are all the books about weight lifting? About martial arts? The illustrated massage books? And where are the study guides for selective service tests on any number of subjects?

Novels by Stephen King vanish, too, and like the supernatural books, perhaps they are spirited away by unseen forces.

And maybe Amos's horse was in the range shelter with him. It is ungenerous of me, but I'm beginning to suspect perfidy in all this. It happens too often. Spruce trees vanish during hunting season, chickens disappear from the flock, library books evaporate from the shelves. I think some people steal.

DECEMBER 1987

Winning the Big Race

February has been an outstanding month for winter sport this year. We see the Olympics on television every night. Closer to home, the 15 kilometer cross-country ski race was held in Heath this weekend.

We didn't miss the TV reporters who went to Calgary for the Olympics instead of to Heath for the ski race. We didn't need anyone wailing that so-and-so was ". . . two seconds behind at the start. A very poor start!" There wasn't much negativism around in Heath on Sunday, despite the savage wind and the cold and icy conditions.

The people in the tight bright colored suits who skied very well and completed the course in an hour or less had a great time. The people in insulated coveralls or heavy corduroys who toiled up the hills and carefully negotiated the downhills had a great time.

And I was there. I wasn't exactly racing. I was celebrating being healthy enough to ski at all. I was behind the pack in the Zen division. Far from cut-throat competition, the people at my end of the race were concentrating on being there, on skiing, not on winning. We apologized when we fell in someone's way, we retrieved each other's loose ski poles, we informed each other that we were "coming through" on those rare occasions when we passed each other.

If we found competition it was in the wind that got beneath our numbered bibs and rattled the plastic as it pushed us from one side of the track to the other. We fell often, from general lack of expertise, and later, from being too tired to ski even as well as we could ski. We slipped back as we tried to climb upward. We took the downward inclines in the snowplow position, or on our backsides, or in an unplanned and undignified sprawl. We rested and saw the glorious views from the top of Heath as we struggled to gain back a little breath and a little more strength.

I was mildly disappointed in reaching the 7½ K mark too late to be able to decide for myself that I was unable to continue. The cut-off time was past; I had to take someone else's word that my race was over.

The Community

I have given up any Olympic dreams I ever had. I have a certificate that says I skied 7½ K; I have bruised knees and probably more bruises in a location I can feel but cannot see.

Monday, Glenn and I went back on the trail and finished the course. We have skied 15 K, more than 9 miles on icy and challenging terrain. It was no Olympic feat, to finish a course in two afternoons that the winner had skied in less than an hour. But we did finish it. The person who finished first wasn't the only winner.

FEBRUARY 1988

Ancestors for Sale

When somebody in our family moved, my parents found themselves with several cardboard boxes filled with old pictures, almost none of them labeled.

We could identify a few: a remembered great-grandmother in long skirt and a blouse with neat tucks and full sleeves; a meat peddler's wagon belonging to a great-grandfather, with white horse standing patiently for the photographer; my grandmother, with a child uncle, in a pose reminiscent of a Mary Cassatt painting; my father, in his youth, astride an already antique high wheel bicycle; the required patriarchal photograph of son, father, grandfather, and great-grandfather, this one dating from the 1880s; and of course the inevitable graduation pictures of everybody in the family who made it through high school.

But there were many we didn't know. They could have

been family, distant in relationship, or distant in time. They could have been friends, somebody else's ancestors. They could have been accidents, found pictures, thrown into the box because, "Let's keep all the photographs together, maybe sometime somebody will recognize this person."

In the box of unknowns there are pictures of little children of both sexes in light colored dresses, pictures of unknown ladies in huge and outrageous hats, pictures of dignified gentlemen in stiff and unsmiling poses. What are we to do with them? Any household has only so much room for the storage of old photographs—barely enough to keep those pictures of family we remember or can place, at the least, somewhere on the family tree.

We could, I suppose, send them to the landfill, hoping that archaeologists of the future will stumble on them and recognize them as treasure trove. But that seems a slim hope to me; I'd like to know someone is getting some enjoyment from them now.

Maybe there is an artist nearby who works with found materials and would like to add an interesting character or two to a collage.

Maybe we should take the unknown portraits to a flea market and sell them beneath a sign lettered "Ancestors for Sale—25 cents." People who have no old pictures could buy them to frame and hang in their homes, thus producing instant family.

For now they sit in a cardboard box in my parents' dining room, with nobody willing to throw them out and nobody willing to give them a home. The old photographs just sit there, waiting for someone to decide their fate.

Evolution of Rubbish Disposal

The three-town landfill dump of Charlemont, Hawley, and Heath is due to close before long. The towns have contracted or are in the process of contracting for some sort of compact-and-haul-away service to deal with rubbish after the dump closes.

Trash is big business these days. There is a lot of trash to dispose of, with any purchased item wrapped in more and more layers of non-degradable stuff, and with the late twentieth century threatening to become known in future archaeological circles as "The Plastic Culture."

You can tell a lot about a society by the way in which it disposes of its rubbish. The small rural towns around here have gone through an evolution from private dump, a steep bank in the woods where cans and bottles and other household refuse were discarded along with worn farm machinery, stripped of any usable parts; to the town dump, a periodically burned site that provided rat shooting as a local sport; to the "sanitary" landfill where acres and acres of land were trenched, filled, and covered in an effort to put rubbish out of sight and hence out of mind. The latest development is compact-and-haul-away, a method whereby the rubbish is deported to another community at great cost. The Town of Rowe's "Refuse Gardens" with plastic security card access is only an atypically ornate form of that latest development.

Neither the unsanitary landfill nor the local dump and burn were clean, safe methods of disposal. Both offered splendid opportunities for pollution. And they smelled.

The primitive haul-it-to-the woods and forget it method certainly wasn't a neat or safe means of disposal, either. You can still wander unsuspectingly into such a site if you have not noticed the warning signs, such as the rusted skeleton of a horse-drawn mowing machine or the blue gleam of an enamel pan half rising above the ground. You realize your error when you bang a shin on a hunk of discarded cast-iron from an old stove. There is real danger of getting cut on a rusty can or broken bottle. Most unbroken bottles were raided from these dumps about ten years ago during the bottle-hunting craze. But even as treasure trove the dumps were usually disappointing. "This one is worth $25!" somebody would say, holding up a dirty brown object with cork still in place and an unknown substance congealed inside. It was like the tales I heard as a child of the astronomical prices one could get for a male three-colored cat. I never met anyone who wanted to buy either old bottles or calico cats.

It seems to be the same syndrome with the haul-it-away rubbish. Supposedly the stuff can be burned to provide energy. You would think, therefore, that somebody would pay money for it, or at least pay for trucking if you gave it to them. That's not what is happening. Rubbish is a liability and it is getting more costly with each change in the way we handle it.

NOVEMBER 1986

Suburbia Comes to the Hill Towns

Land is the big topic of conversation around here these days. Land, its use, its value, is the topic at public meetings and when friends get together.

The Community

People have settled in this small part of Massachusetts for more than 250 years. In the 1800s many left to move west. Now the migration is on again; this time people are moving in. Businesses and houses are being built.

And all these people are talking about the land, what it should be like, how it should be used. Those of us who grew up on farms, with land measured in acres and valued as a way of living; those of us who grew up in measured lots in standard subdivisions, who value rural land for its financial equity; those of us who grew up in clustered rooms in someone else's property in cities and who measure the new house lots in terms of freedom; all of us are different and trying to work out what the future will be for this area. It isn't easy.

We don't even talk the same language. "Open land" is a term the professional planners toss about freely. But to them open land is simply land without houses on it. To a farmer, open land is cleared land, worked for crops or pasture, giving views to Mt. Greylock or to Monadnock or to some southern range.

To the newcomer who has moved to the country, bought a lot, and built a house, open land is privacy, his or her right to a bucolic dream purchased along with the house lot. It is a threat for someone else to be doing the same, especially right across the road! To this person open land is best if heavily wooded to give the most sense of isolation.

To the real estate businessperson open land, whatever its character, is opportunity for development, so that money can be made, and isn't that the American way? Land is valued in dollars and cents.

The new resident has run away from creeping urban sprawl and is frustrated to find it following along. "But this is what we moved away from!" you hear. "We have to stop this!" Town officials sympathize but the same zoning that allowed the first house lot on the country road also permits the second and the third. The town can't apply the laws differently to appease the unhappy.

And the farm folk have their own problems. In our town there was a recent "kitchen meeting" of people who have worked the land. Those people didn't embrace the proposed remedies to the loss of agricultural land. Economics have changed and people who were able to live and work at home, as producers in this society instead of as consumers, were too busy dealing with their grief at the loss of a way of life to consider one more plan that would put control in someone else's hands.

Many people offer an oversimplified solution. Too many people moving in? Change the zoning; require bigger house lots. People who care about land in a truly open state cringe at that one. Most people can't keep two acres mowed and tended. That means the town would develop into little patches of land, each with a lawn surrounded by brush land or scrub woods.

If you own some farm or wood land in a hill town you could sell enough for a building lot for somewhere between 6 and 12 thousand dollars. In today's economy, after you pay the lawyers and real estate people you could put a down payment on a car. In 5 or 6 years the car will be a clunking mass of rust. And where will the land be? It will be lost to its previous use forever.

All this, plus the rising taxes needed to provide services for the increasing population, add up to an atmosphere that could drive out people who have lived here all their lives. Where are the first homes for the young people starting out

The Community

without much cash? Where is the small home with easily tended lot for an elderly couple who may have been productive citizens in a hill town all their lives? New people are moving in—honest and decent people for the most part. The older families may have to go. And suburbia comes to the hill towns.

APRIL 1988

The Death of Pat Smith

Pat Smith died that Sunday at the Heath Fairgrounds, in the ring, while the yoked oxen stood quietly nearby and the other drivers moved uneasily in their concern.

As I came from the truck at a run, my feet flashed up and down, still in the fur-lined bedroom slippers I was wearing when I heard the alarm. Walt outdistanced me easily. There was a group around Pat as he lay on the ground, the sun upon us and a warm wind moving around. I stood for a moment, quickly checking the attendants and their credentials in my head. Susan, nurse practitioner, was applying chest compressions, calmly, firmly, counting to five. Ruth, another nurse practitioner, was monitoring blood pressure and pulse. Tim, an Emergency Medical Technician, was rescue breathing through a plastic mask. Tom, another E.M.T. was there, too. Everyone was more qualified than I.

I stayed where I was, ready to step in if anyone needed relief and I thought about it all. Pat loved an ox draw more than anything, and now he was lying here without breath or heartbeat in the middle of a draw. And I—I had been trained in first-aid—but I felt relief because it looked as if I wouldn't be needed. I turned to Pat's wife, Mary, who stood nearby, watching. Her older daughter was talking to her.

"It will be all right, Ma. See, everybody's helping."

"They're good people," said another woman, "they'll do their best."

"One, two, three, four, five," came the firm count from the circle around Pat.

I reached out and embraced Mary lightly. I don't know what I said. Something about this being Pat's favorite place, that he was among people who cared about him.

"Somebody go for the oxygen respirator."

I felt, rather than saw, Walt leave to get it.

"Where's the ambulance?" someone said.

"It will be here in a moment," I said, although I knew it would be more than a moment. I had been monitoring radio calls and knew that the Charlemont and Shelburne Falls ambulances were tied up at a motorcycle accident on the Mohawk Trail. "Colrain has been called," I said.

There was a stir from around the fallen man. Sue was speaking. "If there is a pulse, I'm not going to continue."

"No, no," everyone agreed. "There's a pulse. Just keep breathing for him." I knew that Pat's heart was working a little now. They wouldn't compress his chest as long as there was any real heartbeat at all. They would just continue to help him breathe. Sheila was there by then and had taken charge of the rescue breathing.

I almost spoke to Mary, still within my arm. I almost said, "They have a pulse now, maybe he'll pull through." But I didn't say that.

The Community

And suddenly they were doing C.P.R. again. The same quiet voice. "One, two, three, four, five." The voice, the pulse, the breath, the voice again. The sequence went on and on.

Mary pulled away from me and went to stand, looking down at Pat. "How will I tell Tina?" she said.

"Now Ma, Tina's a big girl."

"Where's Roy?"

"He's here," I said. Roy was moving fitfully about on the edge of things, going off to handle one of the cattle, coming back to look at the people working on his father, drifting off again.

"He's a big boy, too," May, the daughter, said.

I could see Pat's face. It was a strange ugly blue, an ashy color.

The people in the stands were quiet. There didn't seem to be many of them. Maybe it was because they were so quiet that they seemed so few. I didn't look at them. A group of children huddled around their mother, who was sitting in a lawn chair behind the chain link fence that forms the ring. "This is scary," one of the children said. Silently, I agreed.

"One, two, three, four, five."

I heard Walt return and almost felt the ground move as he dropped the oxygen equipment. He fumbled with the bag. I went to my knees to help him.

"We need the demand valve," Tim said. "Where is it?"

We found it and passed it over.

"One, two, three, four, five. Nothing coming in."

"One, two, three, four, five. That's better."

"One, two, three, four, five. No, it's not working. Can you get a seal with the mask?" The voices were quiet. They sounded conversational. There was no hint of the panic I was feeling. I moved out of the way. I looked at Tim as he adjusted the mask and I wondered if he had a job somewhere. Tim's a decent young man, raised in a farm family. The farm is gone now. He and his father live together in a new house on a hill in north Heath, a house built with money from the sale of their farm. They are quiet people. Tim always comes when someone is sick or hurt.

Steve was bending down helping as his wife, Ruth, monitored blood pressure. He was balancing his infant daughter on his left arm. I moved closer and put a hand on his shoulder.

"I'll take the baby," I said.

He passed her up to me without speaking and I stood holding her against my chest. She snuggled against me, and I wondered how somebody so small could feel so warm. I closed my eyes for a moment, wishing well for us all.

"One, two, three, four, five. That's better."

They had given up on the first respirator and were using a different one. Pat's color was even more unpleasant. Something else was different.

I saw hands gripping his jaw, clamping the mask to the face and holding the head in the proper position, slightly back, airway open. I recognized those hands—Walt was sprawled on the ground, out of everyone else's way and obscured from my sight except for his hands. And I knew those hands, hands that could lift heavy weights, open stubborn jar lids, hands that had touched me in the night, that had lifted many a shaking new calf, and, with less confidence, had supported the heads of my newborn children. Those were the hands clamping the mask to Pat's face. I found myself thinking, "If Pat lives he's going to have a sprained jaw."

"One, two, three, four, five. Good. One, two, three, four, five."

Steve was beside me now and the baby reached for her father. "I wasn't helping much, anyway," he said. "Thank you."

"Thank *you*," I said. "She's beautiful."

A man drove up at high speed in a small green car. He climbed out and walked briskly toward us. He was tall and the sun shone on his blond hair. He stood without speaking, watching the rescuers at work. I didn't know him but I had a feeling he was ready and able to take over if anyone tired. One more to help, I thought.

Then I heard it, still painfully distant but coming closer with every wail.

"The ambulance is coming," I said.

"One, two, three, four, five." The count went on.

The drivers took the oxen from the ring and tied them to the cattle trucks. The siren was getting louder now. I moved the first-aid boxes back against the fence, to allow room for the ambulance.

Now I could see it coming, bouncing at high speed across the rough fairground. The red lights were flashing. It was slowing now, turning into the ring.

It stopped, doors flying open and a small woman giving orders. The count continued without pause. "One, two, three, four, five. Air's going in."

"Listen, everybody who's going to lift—we all lift together on the count of three." The stretcher was beside us now. I moved to lift, but there were so many of us, there was no place for me. I wanted to help so I stood beside Sue, ready to steady her if she was stiff from kneeling. Her hands stayed firmly on Pat's chest. "One, two, *three*," the ambulance woman counted and everyone lifted. Sue never faltered, rising with everyone else, continuing her own count. "One, two, three, four, five. Good."

Pat was in the ambulance and the Heath crew fell back. The blond man climbed in and the doors slammed shut. Sue backed away and her husband reached out to put his arms around her. "Who was it?" she asked.

"Pat Smith," we answered, amazed. Sue knew Pat, but she had worked with such concentration that she never looked at his face.

The ambulance began to move. Out of the corner of my eye I saw a puppy start to ramble into its path. Then I saw Roy reach out to grab it and pull it to safety as the ambulance carried his father away.

A tall young man came up to me, needing to talk about Pat. "He had just hitched on to the stone boat," he said. "It was the first time—a new team. He was so excited. I can't believe it."

I wondered if one of the young team was the little bull calf we had sold Pat a couple of years ago. I stared at the ground—at the opened roll of Lifesavers and the crumpled handkerchief lying there in the place where Pat had been, where people had emptied his pockets in search of medication. The announcer was talking over the loudspeaker, saying that the ox draw would go on, as a tribute for Pat. She said that those drivers who wanted to continue could bring their animals back into the ring. The last thing Pat would have wanted, she said, was to stop an ox draw.

"It was the place Pat would have chosen to die," someone said later. "But he would have preferred to wait until the draw was over."

THE INDIVIDUAL

A Kite to Fly

I bought myself a kite for Mother's Day.

I stood in the toy store in front of the display of kites and tried to select one that was colorful and easy to fly. I rejected one that was shaped and printed to look like a bat. It looked as if it would be hard to fly and, besides, it looked like Halloween and not like spring and Mother's Day.

A salesman approached me. "Can I help you?"

"I'm looking for a kite," I said.

"For someone how old?" he asked.

I thought for a moment, then I looked him in the eye and answered. "Forty-two."

For a brief moment he looked surprised. I continued to look at him firmly. He turned away.

"This kind is easy to fly," he said, pointing to three kites in the classic diamond kite shape.

"I think we can skip the one with the Teddy Bear on it," I said.

In the end I chose a simple diamond in dark blue and green-blue with tail pieces in the same colors. I would have preferred something more colorful. I have seen kites shaped like butterflies and colored in bright gem shades. But this store didn't have great variety. Anyway, the blue diamond looked like a real kite.

For the next week or so I was at work or otherwise occupied whenever the wind came up, so I didn't have a chance to fly the kite. Glenn obligingly offered to test drive

The Individual

it for me one evening when I had to go out. As I drove over the hill, the last thing I saw was the kite, high in the sky. The evening sun caught the mundane shades of blue and brought to them a liveliness that I didn't expect.

I was getting frustrated. It was beginning to look as if I would have no opportunity to get together with the wind before the grass grew to be hay, not to be trampled by kite flyers.

But Sunday evening there was a gusty wind and I was available. I issued polite invitations to go kite flying to the members of my family who were at home. But they were involved in watching "Star Trek Rides Again," or something, on television. So I went alone, which is what I wanted to do anyway.

I had forgotten some things about kite flying, of course. I had forgotten the challenge of getting the kite up there. Someone who has qualified for Mother's Day gifts for more than twenty years is often not adept at running forward while looking backward over one shoulder at a kite and holding up a reel of string. Then when the kite is up in the sky, if the wind is gusty, the kite will circle around and try to make a crash landing, seeming to aim always for the newly plowed ground.

I had forgotten how alive and strong a kite feels on the end of the string, tugging to be free with more force than any fish I ever tried to land. And I had forgotten about the way the string tangles when you least expect it, just like fishing line on a hidden snag, and as difficult to free.

But if I felt uncoordinated and short of breath, I also felt pleasure in the evening outdoors—in the setting sun gleaming on the kite—in the crisp beauty of the mountains, providing a scenic backdrop to my efforts.

The grass is hay now so I won't be trampling it. It doesn't take long when spring finally comes. But I had my delayed Mother's Day gift. For a few minutes last Sunday, it was kite time.

The Individual

MAY 1988

Being Measured for Fitness

My fat's okay. I know because they measured it with pincers—in three different places to make sure they didn't miss any. I'm in the 80th percentile in body fat in my division, females, aged 35–45.

The people at the health club had talked me into having a free fitness evaluation and I was certainly getting evaluated. I hadn't realized how competitive they were about it all. They get excited about percentiles. I wasn't excited about percentiles. I figured half the people who were thinner than I were anorexic or consumptive and the other half were just thin people. I had no desire to beat them out and rise to a higher level of thinness.

They liked my cardiovascular stuff, too. I didn't tell them so, but I thought the measurements were weird. They took a "resting pulse"—after I had gotten up at 7 A.M., done an hour of back exercises, driven 20 miles to civilization, gone into Agway to purchase a new manure fork and then showed up to be evaluated. My pulse was 70, which is quite acceptable, but nobody has a resting pulse after paying $30 for an implement to shovel manure.

The Individual

Then my blood pressure was 90/60. I considered that amazing after the manure fork episode. I realize a low blood pressure is quite stylish in health circles these days, but I figure blood pressure should be high enough so you can tell there is somebody inside. But they liked it and it measured high on the percentiles chart.

I am not in any percentile for bench pressing 35 pounds. I am in disgrace for not being able to bench press 35 pounds. I am not sure why I found this so depressing. I have lived my whole life without ever bench pressing anything before, although I have lifted small children, bales of hay, and many, many stacks of books. I could probably cheerfully live the rest of my life without bench pressing anything. Weight lifting is not on my list of things needed for personal fulfillment. But I was depressed at the failure.

Worse still was the measurement for "trunk flexibility." Without knowing it, I had been in training for this. I have a bad back. As I understand my situation, my vertebrae wander around a bit and, while they finish up in the right place, my muscles get confused trying to follow them. If I don't exercise the muscles every day, some of them stretch tight and some of them just lie there like wet noodles. I had just finished a long session of stretches before I started the journey to town and now I was sitting on the floor with my legs straight out in front of me and a tall woman with real muscles was telling me to gently reach forward as far as I could. The sitting position hurt my back to begin with, but I obediently reached forward. After two trys it was clear that I wasn't going to score high percentiles on this one. I wasn't even on the chart.

After that experience my back ached so I skipped the test where you sit on the floor and somebody holds your feet and you do as many sit-ups as you can as fast as you can. I don't know what that is supposed to measure—insanity, maybe.

There was another cardiovascular test. You step up and down a step for three minutes. Then they listen to your heart to see how soon it slows down. Mine had gone back to 108 thumps after a minute so that was a good percentile. They liked the statistic and that test didn't hurt my back so we were all pleased.

It was certainly an unusual experience to be evaluated. I know my fat's okay and my cardiovascular system is working even though I can't lift 35 pounds or bend my body. At least they didn't tell me I'm too short, although maybe the tall woman with the muscles thought so.

OCTOBER 1988

A Box of Procrastination

Under my bed sits a box of procrastination. It has been there all winter and spring and I think it will be there all summer, too. We have had plenty of challenging situations these past few months. The unusual projects seemed to force my attention and get done, but not so some of the more usual complications of daily life. A project I didn't feel like doing got tossed in an old cardboard box to wait until I felt up to doing it. The box became older and more tired looking as time went by. And it got fuller.

The income tax information sat in the box for months

until mid-April when I had no choice but to fill out the forms. The same thing happened with Glenn's college application stuff. He is as bad a procrastinator as I am and besides, you can't fill out a financial aid form until you have done the income tax.

The box contains a button from my winter coat. I wanted to have the people at the dry cleaner sew it on but the woman was shocked by the suggestion. "You don't want to pay us just to sew on *one button!*" she said. Oh, yes I do, I thought, but I meekly agreed with her and went out, leaving the coat to be cleaned and with the button in my pocket. The two have not yet got together again. So the button sits in the box with the unanswered correspondence and other stuff I have chosen to jettison temporarily from my life.

There is a particularly fat envelope in the box of procrastination that contains a book proposal returned from a second publisher on the day before Christmas. I need to reorganize and expand it and send it out again, but still it sits. Every time I look at it I remember how I felt when it came. I was frantic with holiday preparations and uncomfortable with back pain. I didn't need rejection too. Of course no editor sends rejection slips to make writers feel bad, I tell myself. I wonder if I believe it. I don't think any writer really believes it.

There are three months' bank statements in the box. Another one came the other day. It hasn't made the journey into the box yet, but I'm sure it will land there. I opened it up and took out the canceled checks, which looked vaguely familiar, then left it on the bedside stand to age or something. I don't feel like doing math today. There will be a time when I will have to reconcile those things but today isn't it.

The Individual

There are days when I decide to tackle the box. I clear a surface and take everything out and make organized piles. This pile is business and involves finding the checkbook and the calculator. This pile simply needs me to sit down and write letters. To deal with this pile I will need to turn detective and find out my social security number or the date of my last tetanus shot or something equally obscure. Sometimes I do one thing. Sometimes I even do two or three things. Then I feel virtuous and in control. But it doesn't last. Soon the box is full again. I figure it will take a year to clear out the leftover obligations from the last six months.

MAY 1987

Chimes of Great Resonance

He seemed to be a nice man and his wind chimes were lovely. They were made of gleaming copper tubing cut to different lengths and wired together, along with chunks of smooth polished cherry wood. He swung his arm and set them ringing. The sound was a mellow blending of different tones that seemed to echo softly in the enclosed hall. I loved them.

I looked at the price tag: $149. I didn't like them as much as I had a moment before. I asked why they cost so much.

They were special wind chimes, he told me. Spiritual ones, created out of his years of study of Eastern religions and his experience in psychic counseling.

The Individual

He was a healer, he said, and these were healing chimes. They healed the earth. The chimes, he said "create a convergent harmonic relationship between the heavenly and earthly energies."

That's what he said.

It seems that the chimes act like bird feeders to attract primitive spiritual beings and good earth energies. Each time they ring it is like sending a prayer to heaven.

I liked him and I liked the chimes, and I would probably have liked the spiritual beings and good earth energies, too. But I didn't like the $149 price tag. So I thanked him and accepted his literature which told about healing the earth with spirituality. And I went on my way.

I thought of all the different kinds of wire I must have at home: thin copper wire that Walt uses to fix the mysterious innards of electric motors, rugged electric fence wire, and even old coat hangers. We used to have some dynamite wire about, but that was years ago. I thought of how inexpensive copper tubing is, compared to $149. There are always pieces of old board lying about. I could cut, sand and polish hunks of used lumber, cut copper tubes, and make my own wind chimes to hang on the porch.

And nobody would know that they weren't special spiritual wind chimes developed after years of psychic study to heal the earth.

Nobody at my house expects psychic study from me or prayer from a wind ornament, anyway. My family would be surprised, stepping out on the porch, to meet up with spiritual beings and good earth energies.

So maybe I'll make my own chimes and we'll see what happens. My chimes can hang on the porch and glow in the morning sunlight and when the wind comes they can make their own gentle sound.

APRIL 1988

The Individual

Marking Pages

I spent a long time the other day searching for some information I had scratched on a used library catalog card, a dummy card, as we call such things in the trade. I stirred the debris on my desk and looked through my accumulation. I was getting discouraged. I had thought of ruling off the desk work surface into quadrants and sectors and perhaps even mapping out the strata like an archaeological dig when my colleague, who needed the information, said, "Never mind, it will be easy enough for me to just look it up again."

But she didn't have to repeat my research because I found the file card. I had used it for a bookmark in a fat loose-leaf volume of reproducible art for libraries.

Some people mark their places in books with strips of tooled leather or delicate metal clips or neat paper bookmarks with pictures of flowers or "a prayer for the day." I own some bookmarks. You always get a paper one at the bookstore when you buy a book. We hand them out every day at the library. I use them to promote reading-discussion series or other library programs. A relative made me a beautiful one for Christmas one year—cross-stitched on linen with a matching eyeglass case.

But I don't use that kind of bookmark. I use 3×5 file cards with important information written on them; I use those subscription cards blown into and always falling out of magazines; I use grocery lists, old and current; I use bank statements—the account won't balance anyhow; and I use unpaid bills.

I have had a good supply of unpaid bills lately because Glenn incurred some medical debts in a bicycle accident this summer and the health insurance people have been in no hurry to pay. The radiologists, the doctors, the two emergency rooms, and other assorted healers have been writing to me threatening to repossess the kid. The best thing to do with those kind of bills, the flimsy tissue paper and carbon sandwich things that tear when you open them, is not to open them. Simply fold in half and use for a bookmark. Every month or two you send a collection of them off to the insurance company with a note asking if they wouldn't like to pay. There are always plenty left over to use for bookmarks.

Perhaps there will be a time in my life when there will be a real bookmark nearby when I need it and I will actually use it to mark a place in a book. Maybe I will even be reading a book that has enough class so I will think to use the hand-embroidered linen one. But that is later. This is now and what I find is what I use—for bookmarks, anyway.

NOVEMBER 1987

A Person Defined by Numbers

Figuring out who you really are is a task that emerges again and again at different stages in life. It is probably part of the exploring process of a baby, playing with fingers and toes; it is certainly a big piece of the trauma that goes by the name of adolescence; and I am beginning to think it has a part in middle age, too.

You know, in middle age, who you were; now you are trying to figure out how to be you, the way you find yourself today—with hair graying, or balding perhaps, with figure spreading or simply sinking to new lows. You find you sometimes can't move as fast, do as much, keep up the younger pace. This is me?

No matter at what age you are trying to deal with who you are now, you don't need to hassle with outside forces pushing their own concerns about who you are.

There is the Registry of Motor Vehicles, for example. They have recently had a publicity campaign saying that they are going to be nicer to people. Maybe they are, but not when it comes to answering the question, "Who are you?" Whatever you do, try not to lose your driver's license. After dealing with them on that matter, you probably won't know your own name.

Dan lost his driver's license. So he went to the Registry, twenty miles away, armed with birth certificate, bank book and library card—the same ID he used when he got the license. No, they would not issue a replacement license. He needed a passport, which he didn't have, or a yearbook with his picture in it, something he has but did not happen to have in his hip pocket that day.

Failing all that, he needed someone over twenty-five to

The Individual

vouch for his identity. He had to go to the library and kidnap a librarian friend to return to the Registry with him to present her ID and sign a paper testifying that he is, in fact, he.

My sister Ruth has the same problem. She showed up at the Registry with a picture ID that she was sure would suffice.

No such luck! It was not the Registry's own ID. Why would they believe someone else's? There was no friend or relative available to help her that day, so she has to go back.

Her problem is complicated by the fact that she was unwise enough to change her name when she married. Thus her birth certificate and her yearbook will not help unless she also has a marriage certificate to testify to the transition from her birth name to her married one.

Speaking of red tape, take the IRS. Take it as far away as it will go. The IRS is not merely content with a name, social security number, spouse name and spouse's social security number on a form 1040. They also want the same information painstakingly supplied on any other form a person might file.

That means for a farmer the need to write in this same boring information on Schedule F, Farm Income and Expenses; Schedule B, reporting the interest from your savings account; Schedule 4797, if you should sell some cows; Schedule D, because why should the IRS have you fill out one form about selling cows if they can make you fill out two; Schedule 4136, Computation of Credit for Federal Tax on Gasoline and Special Fuels; and Schedule C, if you should make a small income writing stuff for the local paper.

Now, I am a person who has never memorized her Social

Security Number. It is just not interesting enough to remember. I always have to look it up. Looking it up once is enough, I figure; I shouldn't have to look it up and copy it over again and again.

The Individual

I may not always know exactly who I am, but I know a Social Security Number is a reductive way to summarize me.

The IRS is short on wisdom in this respect. And the Registry of Motor Vehicles even less wise.

It seems to me that we go through enough soul-searching in figuring out who we are in the larger sense, without dealing with the bureaucracy's petty demands to know who we are in the smallest.

MARCH 1988

The Art and Science of Walking

It started about three months ago when I decided to fit a walk into each day's schedule. I simply went out my door and around the block. Of course, "the block" in Heath is a two and a half mile triangle filled with ups and downs of terrain, bordered by some of the most stunning scenery you could find around here, and in winter blasted by strong winds.

It seemed a challenging course of action since I was not physically fit. I would slowly push my body for the first mile and a half, then settle quietly to my knees to breathe for a while before plodding on.

The Individual

I made the mistake of mentioning the project to my doctor. "Two and a half miles a day!" He seemed delighted. Then—"Make it five."

By this time I wished I had kept my mouth shut. It didn't seem to me as if my body wanted to walk five miles. Certainly not five Heath miles. But "the block" was easier to walk now and I was enjoying the opportunity to stop and talk with neighbors I encountered along the route. The experience seemed therapeutic so I pushed ahead to four and occasionally five miles.

Then came the complication. "Since you are walking so much I want you to get some Walking Shoes," said the doctor.

What does he mean, thought I, hiking boots?

But no, he didn't mean hiking boots bought at the Salvation Army. He meant special sneakers sold at ridiculously high prices for the sport of Walking. Walking as a sport was a new concept for me and the shoes looked just a bit weird. Diagrams in the store showed how specially constructed they were, like steel-belted radial tires. So I bought the shoes and tried to forget the whole existence of Walking as a sport.

It was not to be. "You should read this article," said a friend at work. "Since you're walking so much now."

The article was all about Walking. It seemed I was supposed to be wearing a shiny skintight outfit with stripes on the legs when I went Walking. And the shoes I had bought were all wrong. The magazine people could suggest a dozen different brands, all of which seemed to have cost a hundred dollars or so more than mine.

I had also done my "conditioning" all wrong. I usually think of conditioning as something that is done for the hair.

But this conditioning meant that I should have started Walking in much smaller distances than I had. As for uphills, why, according to their chart of grades and distances, I would have to have been in training five weeks before I would be allowed to Walk to the mailbox to get the mail! I shouldn't have simply Walked out the door. I should have done "warm-up exercises" first. Then I should have Walked for a while and then taken my pulse. When my pulse reached a certain point on a chart that looked more difficult to follow than my high school logarithm charts, I should have gotten down to Walking—fast, four miles an hour. And no stopping to look for wild flowers or to talk with the neighbors or to take a drink from Whittemore Spring. When I got home I should do more exercises.

I decided to pretend I didn't know about the article. I didn't want to wear a shiny tight suit. Besides, it is difficult to find my pulse. And how do you calculate miles per hour when the road is going up and down hill all the time? A slower mountain climbing Heath mile is more difficult than a fast flatland mile in the city.

But most of all, I don't want to get that intense about the whole thing. I don't want to hunt for my pulse and time my rate of speed. I'm not trying to prove anything aerobic. All I want is to feel well and to be reacquainted with my neighborhood.

So if you see me on the road, I'm not Walking. I'm just going for a walk.

MAY 1987

All Will Be Well

Mid-January comes near the beginning of the calendar year but for many of us, it represents the wakeful and troubled 3 A.M. of our seasons. While a few people are gliding through the first month, enjoying winter sports, social doings, and fulfilling their New Year's resolutions without a tremor, others of us are suffering the January cough left from December's flu, general post-holiday depression, or grief from untimely loss. The weather is bad and housebound people are getting edgy. Those who must go out are finding nasty traveling conditions. Some days it just means a longer time getting to work and getting home. Sometimes it means the aggravation of a minor accident and the inconvenience of a disabled automobile. For others the accidents are more severe. Ambulance crews are busy this month. Fire departments are responding to more chimney fires and hoping to avoid worse ones.

On the national scene we have heard bad news for a while. We've heard of lawlessness, immorality, and irresponsibility on high levels. The president is mending after unmentionable surgery which has been mentioned too often and in too much detail for most of us.

Winter seems to me to be more than a minor tribulation. It represents a confrontation of life and death. Usually we make it through. In the words of the folk song

> . . . *Let the winter come and go.*
> *All shall be well again, I know.*

I find January the most difficult month—and yet, strangely, one full of hope. If the days are short and dark, and they surely are, each short dark day is a tiny bit longer.

The Individual

If we have passed the cheerful holidays of December, we at least are able to get on with some heartfelt grumbling without fear of putting a blight on someone else's joy. If we find bitter weather stressful, at least we have something else to look forward to.

Groundhog Day is coming. We will be allowed to talk about spring. There are ski races and winter carnivals in the meantime. Maple Sugar time is coming. Farmers tell of plodding on snowshoes to set sap buckets, and a few weeks later walking in sneakers on bare ground to pull them.

It is a time to think of healing—not for forgetting the winter's deep griefs and temporary distresses, but for learning from them and growing because of them. January is a time of testing and renewing faith. There will be a spring. All shall be well again.

JANUARY 1987

THE NATURAL ORDER

The Bird of Spring

The weather is changing. Sap has been running in the trees and people have been boiling maple syrup. There have been days of snow and days of rain. There have been cold days, too. Now and then we have had a rare and precious day of warmth, a day when we have dressed ourselves in merely medium-density clothes and gone outdoors to turn our faces toward the sun and we have been able to feel real warmth.

I've been looking for the spring birds and I have found them, but they are not the traditional first birds of my earlier springs. I have seen no robins and bluebirds. But the wild turkeys are back. They spent the summer and autumn here in the hills, then fled to the more balmy climate of upper Charlemont for the winter. They've been around for about three weeks now, leaving their thin cross-shaped tracks in the woods and fields. The biggest group I've seen had seven individuals. It was nothing like the tribes of up to two dozen that made their self-appointed rounds late last year.

A turkey is not the usual harbinger of spring, but I think it is an appropriate one. A turkey is large and brown and seems ungainly—until you try to catch up with one and realize how fast the creature is actually running.

Early spring is large too, the longest season. And next to deepest winter it is the most difficult to bear. It is a brown season, taking our dirt roads from ice to mud and back again. There is nothing graceful about early spring. It gives

The Natural Order

off hints of mild weather to come—the shy bloom of a clump of crocuses in a sheltered spot; a patch of green grass; the productive steam rising from a sugar house. Then comes a surly day of strong wind and spitting snow, followed by a night of clear and bitter cold. Spring, like the turkey, is elusive. Try to catch hold of spring! Plan a weekend of skiing and the hills will turn to ice or mud. Try to get together with a friend to walk around the "block" (two and a half miles of strenuous scenery, around here) and the day will turn to arctic chill. Decide that the weather is doubtful, a good day to do the income tax, and the sun will come through the clouds to confound you with warmth. Early spring is a time for planning nothing, especially nothing to do with weather.

I find early spring the turkey of all seasons, contrary and unpredictable, homely and clumsy. I am glad it is here. Each day has a little more light. There are signs, elusive, uncoordinated and ugly, but still signs that sometime there will be a real spring and later, say by July, we will have summer.

MARCH 1988

Treatise on the Pig Potato

I garden for food but I'm always finding something else. I learn a lot, even if I knew it the year before but forgot somehow over the long dead winter. I find out about the behavior of weather, of dirt, of stray livestock and even

The Natural Order

about the character of the plants themselves. Each season brings small new clues to the order of things.

In the spring I plant a few seed potatoes to gain many for food. Potatoes are a rich crop even before harvest. They sprout early, each tiny eye on the piece of buried potato becoming a new plant with crinkled foliage of a deep and ever amazing green. I can tell something is happening in the garden when the potatoes come up.

Then comes the time to confront bugs, ravenous yellow striped critters, doomed to be dropped by hand into a can of used motor oil, or blasted by spray, or smashed between rocks, according to the ecological convictions of the gardener. The bug destruction goes on all summer, between weeding and hilling. And the plants grow and flower and keep their secrets about the state of the crop of tubers developing below.

Digging potatoes is a treasure hunt. Like the earlier episodes in the season of the potato plant, it brings its rewards—and not always the expected ones. It starts with a mild fall day, a glorious afternoon to spend in the garden, preparing for wilder weather to come. It is time to rummage in the woodshed to find an instrument for excavation, to take from the nail the long-handled potato hook with the four bent tines and lug it, along with assorted containers, to the garden and the long rows of weary, mature potato plants. I grab a wilted plant and pull it up, shaking loose the tubers clinging to its roots. Then I carefully insert the hook and rake through the hill, pulling out the rest of the potatoes. The potatoes roll out of the hill, thrown from the clasp of the hook into the September light. That's when I examine my treasure to discover how many potatoes I have grown, and how big they are. There are all sizes and all

The Natural Order

shapes. Some are smooth and round, some touched with green where the tops had poked above the ground to be colored by the sunlight, some are sliced by the hook, or show scars from an unsuspected gnawing rodent.

I regard the biggest potatoes with pride—special baking potatoes destined for the Thanksgiving table. I feel a measure of self-satisfaction over the large potatoes and even the average ones. I gather medium-sized potatoes with the usual yankee practicality, and small ones with my own thrift. But the smallest, those that fall through the wire egg basket that serves as harvest container, bring a philosophical gift. I gather them with care because they represent one of the garden's small lessons.

Farmers call the littlest ones "pig potatoes" because of the custom of turning the pigs into the garden at the end of the season to finish off vegetables not worth harvesting. I never used to gather pig potatoes, even when we had no pigs to clean the garden. A potato the size of a marble or even a golf ball doesn't seem an important affair on a busy farm.

And yet, not long ago Walt and I decided to honor an anniversary by dining out at a nearby restaurant of great repute, and of great expense. There, on the menu, and subsequently on our plates, we found "sauteed baby new potatoes." Our old friends, the pig potatoes, each had a strip of peel delicately removed from its middle and had been cooked in butter and garnished with chopped parsley. I have thought of pig potatoes differently since then.

Tradition in farm families dictates that, when saving potatoes for next year's seed, small ones be discarded. Supposedly, if you planted small potatoes you would get small potatoes. But I've meditated on pig potatoes now and I've decided that can't be true. Potatoes are tubers, pieces of bloat from the root of the plant. As such, each potato is a clone of the parent plant. A pig/gourmet potato is genetically identical in seed quality with any super baking potato from the same hill.

At the local fair, long wooden tables are crowded with produce from garden and field. There are classes for the biggest vegetable, the largest pumpkin, the tallest stalk of field corn. I can't recall ever seeing a class judged on the smallest. Yet size isn't always the winning factor. An exhibitor displaying four large potatoes and one small in a plate class wouldn't win the blue ribbon. The criteria in a plate class are uniformity and general attractiveness, not outstanding size.

The lesson in the pig potato is that everything has its place in the scheme of things. And often the same small thing has more than one right place in that order.

When there are hungry swine to be fed on a busy farm, pig potatoes are economical feed. Prepared with care and honored with a fancy name, pig potatoes are fit to serve at an elegant restaurant. When I cut the seed potatoes into small pieces, each with two or three eyes, and plant them, when I pull the weeds and murder the bugs, when I hoe a mound of dirt around each deep green plant, creating the hill that nests the tubers—my goal is still the baking potato. But I gather up pig potatoes now. And I look at them with a new awareness. Pig potatoes are food for thought.

OCTOBER 1986

Something is Missing

It doesn't look like much. Just a big dead tree fallen over a stone wall. There is green mold on the bark and the red wood is soggy to the touch. To someone who knows, it represents an important relic in the history of the woods, an honorable contributor to our own history, and a victim to human disturbance of the natural order.

The fallen tree is a chestnut. In the nineteenth century Longfellow brought it literary popularity in his poem about the village blacksmith. But it had already earned respect from the farmers and builders. Chestnut wood is light and strong, with a tight grain. It can be split easily but is difficult to break. If you put a rock in a post hole for drainage, a chestnut fence post will last nearly as long as a locust one. The stone wall holds the wreck of the tree off the damp loam of the woods floor and keeps it from disintegrating beyond recognition.

My house is framed with chestnut. In the attic and cellar you can see the handhewn beams that form the skeleton of the house. The house moves and whispers when the wind blows and creaks loudly during a storm. It seems alive. There is nothing of the rigid resistance of the modern house.

In some places, you can still find young chestnut trees struggling to bring back the species. They grow only so big before the blight attacks and kills them. It was the blight that killed the big tree lying in ruin over the stone wall. People brought in foreign chestnut trees from the Orient and the new species carried a disease the American chestnut couldn't fight.

One year a young tree in our woods matured enough to

bear fruit before it died. The large nuts were covered with spines like sea urchins. They looked like tiny curled porcupines. I had never seen anything like them before. The old tree and the others of its generation died before I was born. Still the young ones keep trying to live.

I grieve for the American chestnut tree. It is not just blind nostalgia for the "spreading chestnut tree" of Longfellow's time, the huge shade tree I have never seen; nor is it mere practical regret for valuable lumber. In the passing of that big tree we have another small gap in our world. Something important is missing.

JULY 1986

The Traveling Blossom

There is something odd about lady's-slippers. These wild flowers are difficult to find but not, I think, because of their comparative rarity.

You can find a lady's-slipper on a day in early June, admire its delicate pink bloom rising above the two large leaves, note its location in your mind, and resolve to return to visit it next year. The following year you return and the plant is nowhere to be found. Perhaps on another day, hiking in another part of the woods entirely, you will spot a lady's-slipper where none had grown before.

I think the lady's-slipper, or moccasin flower, travels. It's not as if it had an excuse. This is no fungi that reproduces by windblown spores. It's just an ordinary plant with a

The Natural Order

tuberous root, a member of the orchid family. But it moves, mysteriously, I think. Or maybe it is my mind that can't keep track, from one year to another, of where the wild flowers are. But that doesn't seem to be a problem with trillium or violets or swamp pink or even jack-in-the-pulpit. Only the lady's-slipper is consistently elusive.

I found one the other day, on the side of a logging road that leads to the brook where the old sugar house stood. At the next opportunity I dragged an only mildly interested spouse off to see it because there hadn't been any lady's-slippers there before. We were but a short way toward the goal when he said, "What's wrong with looking at *those* lady's-slippers?"

There were eight of them on the bank on the other side of the road, growing in the shelter of the pines. They hadn't been there before, either.

After we admired the flowers we went on to check the ski trail and look for lumber trees and potential firewood. We covered a lot of territory before we returned home. We also saw eighteen lady's-slippers, all in places where I never saw any before. It is a good year for orchids, I guess. I wonder how many will be there next year. And if they aren't there, I wonder where they will have gone and why.

JUNE 1988

A Wolf at the Door

Sunday at noontime a wild canine loped by, coming from the north, and traveled the length of the field in full view of our buildings. It stayed in the open, shunning the protection of the woods to the east, ignoring people and cattle alike as we all stood to watch.

There is controversy about such animals. One faction insists that all of them are "coy-dogs," the result of the mingling of feral dogs with a wild coyote population. Another group says that at least some of them are a new breed, the Eastern wolf.

There was nothing coy about the animal we saw this weekend. It was the least shy of any wild dog I've ever seen. It didn't move with the usual run of a domestic dog, nor the familiar trot of the fox. It didn't have the jogging pace I've come to associate with "coy-dog." This beast loped. It had somewhere to go and was on its way in a distinct and efficient manner. And it was big. I watched it go and thought, "That's a wolf."

The wolf is at the door in a more symbolic way for many west county families. The traditional means of earning our way seem to be fading out. The loss of manufacturing jobs like those at the closed factories of Kendall and Glassine have made many search for other kinds of work. Dairying is in economic distress here, in a district that agriculture experts rate without value for any other kind of farming.

And here, too, there is disagreement about what is going on. Some people feel that the hill towns will turn into bedroom communities, with all open land cut into suburban lots to house a large population of commuters. Others think we can adapt and work our way out of the economic predicament by using our wits to develop new local business.

I think we can. If there is something we are not lacking, it is people of character. And it will take both stubbornness and flexibility to work out new ways of living. The wolf, traditionally a symbol of disaster, has shown up in our territory in the form of a new species, demonstrating its stubbornness and adaptability. I think we should be encouraged, not frightened, by it.

MAY 1986

The Rebellion of an Old House

My house is 200 years old and it needs fixing. I suppose it is natural that something so old should need repair, but why is it that the newer parts of the house are in the worst shape?

The plumbing and heating modernizations are constantly creaking and moaning, if not outright leaking. The ell added to the northeast end of the saltbox moves around with the weather, like the oceans with the tides, and needs attention with building jacks and other support systems. It was probably added on at the turn of the century, not at all ancient enough to be worn out, and I know it was remodeled since then.

The porch was built in the 1940s—in living memory, in fact. It is the carpenter's good fortune to be dead now, because I would speak to him about the quality of his work if he were still around. One end started to lean and when we investigated we found serious deficiencies with the skeleton of the thing.

Now I will admit that the outstanding sag in the floors toward the middle of the house is a fault related to the original construction. There was once a massive chimney there, with fireplaces on three sides. But the problem is not in what the pioneers built; it is in what their followers altered. For the chimney was removed and replaced with a smaller one to meet the needs of the latest technology. That was the First Wood Stove Era, in the nineteenth century. It brought two stovepipe holes hacked in the paneled wall of the living room.

Without the big chimney that provided a central support, the house started to fold in on itself, crumpling inward like an apple dumpling. So, to shore it up, more strange construction was done. What you see when you stand in the cellar and look up at the northeast joists and beams is, in carpenter's terms, "a cobbled-up mess."

With the chimney removed, there was space in the middle of the house, so someone decided to make a more direct route from the lower attic to the top one, cutting through the two main carrying beams in the process of building the stairway.

Then there are bathrooms. The house didn't have one when it was built. Later, there was an outhouse built off the woodshed at the side of the ell. Flowers still do well in this fertile location. When I moved into the house, a bathroom had been built into the ell. But, as I mentioned before, the ell moves around. This heaving made gaps in the walls. It got cold in there. Then the plumbing leaked, from all the motion, no doubt, and rotted the floor. So we moved the bathroom to the center space that had contained the original chimney, even though we had been warned that had been tried before. Mildew does well there.

Now mind you, I am not saying, "They don't build them like they used to." That's too simple. A house well built in 1780 is a good house. A house well built in the 1980s is a good house, too. The problem is that people expect unhar-

The Natural Order

monious things of a house. People thought our house could do without its central chimney. They expected it to accept new-fangled plumbing and heating never dreamed of by the builders and they expected it to tolerate an ell added here and a porch hitched on there. The house is rebelling against it. As I said, it needs fixing.

NOVEMBER 1986

A Pumpkin on a Fence Post

Last fall, my neighbors put a pumpkin on a fence post to add a pleasant harvest touch to the landscape. After a while, the snow fell and covered it. Instead of an autumn scene, it looked as if one fence post was longer and more top-heavy than the others. I forgot about the pumpkin.

Then the brief January thaw came and I noticed the pumpkin wearing a darker and more mellow color than its bright orange coat of the fall. But it was still recognizable as a pumpkin on a fence post.

More winter came, of course, and then the first rough beginnings of spring. The last few weeks have brought big changes in weather, with the usual freezes and thaws of sugaring time and the usual wet and warm and wet and cold cycles. There have been changes in the pumpkin, too. First its color became more and more blurred. Then it became shorter and wider, and finally it developed a distinct list, moving lower and lower on one side of the fence post.

> The Natural Order

My family began to share my interest in the pumpkin, making bets on when it would finally fall off the post.
"Is it still there?"
"It's still there."
We didn't think it would last through the weekend. But it did. It lasted through that weekend and the next. Everyone lost the bet; weeks passed and the pumpkin remained in a slouched posture on the fence post. It was no longer recognizable as a pumpkin; as it moved further and further down the fence post it looked less and less like a round object, and more and more like something fluid poured over the post and remaining there in defiance of gravity.

My family moved on to saner and more legitimate concerns; I was left alone in my interest in the neighbor's disintegrating vegetable.

On Saturday I squished my way through soggy grass to the fence post to investigate this tenacious object. I extended a finger to touch it, ready to draw back at the first feel or odor of decay. My fingernail tapped on a hard surface. The pumpkin had mummified. No wonder, even in its flowing position, it had stuck to the post!

Several days later, after a weekend of alternating warmth and rain, I again tested the wonder pumpkin. Now its hide felt like rubber and it gave way a bit against the pressure of my finger. Still it clung to the post.

It seems to me that the pumpkin spent the worst part of the winter, the part most threatening to humans, in a state of frozen preservation. Now, with warmer weather, it is beginning to yield. But it has not yet given way. I think it is waiting for the soil temperature to rise, waiting for the right time to fall, its mess of dried and rotting flesh sheltering seeds. If the timing is right, if nature's bet is more accurate than ours had been, the seeds will take root and next summer there will be pumpkin vines spreading out in all directions from the fence post.

APRIL 1988

A Place Where Life Was

It's a sunny spot in a tangle of woods, now accessible only by a logging road nearly a mile from a maintained road. The trees are not big but they look wild enough. You have to look closely to spot the elderly apple trees here and there, and the lilac and elderberry.

Stones carefully moved and laid into a wall, bricks fired nearby and built into a chimney now crumbled into an earthen pile, a narrow one-horse road carved into the side of the steep hill and reinforced with stone—they are the few clues remaining in this place that was once a farm and is now woodland. The barn was large, even by today's standards. You can trace its dimensions in stone walls more straight and true than those which support my house.

This was home to somebody once. The land that is grown to brush and light woods was once carefully tended field, and the deeper woodland was pasture for cattle and for sheep. Along the edge of the gap, where the quiet brook pours downward, growing louder in sound and faster in speed as it falls, there was a mill of some sort. I can't tell from the stone foundations if it was a water-powered sawmill or a gristmill or if light manufacturing was done here. And no one seems to remember. But during the spring run-off when the quiet brook rose and roared, something happened here. People were as busy here as they were in the sunny spot where the house foundation now lies half-buried in sod and brambles.

The Natural Order

Things have changed and are changing still. In the early part of the last century these hill towns supported populations much larger than now and most of the land was cleared and productive. This was a time of large families crowded into few houses. Now the population is growing again. Little land is farmed, most is woodland, but more and more is being developed into house lots for a larger population, living in smaller homes with their smaller families.

And in the woods the old foundation hole waits quietly to be rediscovered.

APRIL 1987

A Horse Again

There is a horse living at my place these days. He's here on approval. In a way, I'm "test driving" him. I think I'll keep him.

I haven't had a horse for twelve years. Commander's arrival signifies a kind of healing for me. On April 12, 1976, we suffered a barn fire that destroyed our farm buildings, our entire dairy herd, and my mare and colt. Until now, I hadn't wanted to have a horse again. Now, it feels like it's time.

The Natural Order

Commander, the new horse, is a Standardbred. At twelve years old he is long retired as a harness racer.

He is a bay—which means that he is the color of a batch of good, rich fudge—and he is about 14½ hands tall. That means when I stand beside him, his withers (the high part of his shoulder) reach to my eye level. That makes us a good match because Commander is smaller than your average horse and I'm smaller than your average woman.

I've forgotten a lot about horses in the last twelve years. I need to learn the most simple things all over again. The first time I rode Commander, somebody else put the saddle on.

I was alone when I rode him next and I found that no matter how I pondered, I could not remember how to tie the knot to cinch a western saddle. The more I thought the bigger the mess I made.

Commander stood quietly while I tried again and again. Finally my mind wandered, I stopped paying attention and my fingers tied the knot. They went up, then down, up through the ring and in back, then forward and down through the loop. I couldn't do it consciously. Twelve years after my mare Joyce, and her colt, Zeke, died in the fire, my hands remembered a knot and I rode a horse again.

It was windy that first day I rode Commander alone, here at the farm. I was nervous because a horse will often respond to a windy day by becoming playful like a kitten. Unlike the kitten, a horse is a large beast and I was out of practice in controlling one.

But Commander was reputed to be a gentle horse and, after all those years I wanted to ride again. So, awkwardly, I put on the tack and even more awkwardly (I have gotten stiffer in the last twelve years), I mounted and we headed into the woods on an old logging road.

The Natural Order

There was a birch log lying beside the road, almost luminous in its whiteness against the shadowed woods. Commander snorted, his breath coming out in a throaty whistle, as if to say, "What's that?"

"It's a birch log," I said.

He snorted again, more quietly, as if to answer, "Oh."

A wild turkey ran out of some bushes and off into the deeper woods. Commander stood still, ears up, and watched it. "It's a turkey," I said. "We have a lot of them."

"Oh," he seemed to answer.

And that's the way it went, that first day. We were getting acquainted with each other. I was relearning the fundamentals of riding and Commander was learning about a new rider and new territory. I wanted him to wade through a shallow brook; he wasn't sure that was such a good idea. He wanted to settle into a bone-jarring pace; I wanted him to forget the race track and use a less painful gait.

We negotiated and things worked out. We saw a deer in the field on the way home. It saw us and bounded into the woods. Commander only watched. The wind blew. Everything felt right. It was a good day.

SEPTEMBER 1988

Typeset in Linotype Janson
by The Composing Room of Michigan, Inc.
Grand Rapids, Michigan
Printed and Bound by McNaughton & Gunn Inc.
Ann Arbor, Michigan

Book Design: Jeanne Ray Juster
Production Associate: Patricia Czepiel